Marek Ryś

Colour illustrations by Thierry Vallet

Hawker
HURRICANE

Published in Poland in 2015
by STRATUS s.c.
Po. Box 123,
27-600 Sandomierz 1, Poland
e-mail: office@mmpbooks.biz
for
Mushroom Model Publications,
3 Gloucester Close,
Petersfield,
Hampshire GU32 3AX
e-mail: rogerw@mmpbooks.biz

© 2015 Mushroom Model
Publications.
http://www.mmpbooks.biz

All rights reserved. Apart from any fair dealing for the purpose of private study, research, criticism or review, as permitted under the Copyright, Design and Patents Act, 1988, no part of this publication may be reproduced, stored in a retrieval system, or transmitted in any form or by any means, electronic, electrical, chemical, mechanical, optical, photocopying, recording or otherwise, without prior written permission. All enquiries should be addressed to the publisher.

**ISBN
978-83-63678-88-3**

Second revised edition

Editor in chief
Roger Wallsgrove

Editorial Team
Bartłomiej Belcarz
Artur Juszczak
Robert Pęczkowski
Dariusz Karnas
James Kigthly

Colour drawings
Thierry Vallet
Karolina Hołda

Scale plans
Marek Ryś
Dariusz Karnas

DTP & Layout
Stratus

Printed by
Drukarnia Diecezjalna,
ul. Żeromskiego 4,
27-600 Sandomierz
www.wds.pl
marketing@wds.pl

PRINTED IN POLAND

Table of contents

Acknowledgements 2
Introduction 3
Fury Monoplane 4
Hurricane 6
Prototype K5083 6
Versions 10
   Mk I 10
   Mk I (late series) 15
   Official and unofficial Mk I Variations 19
   Mk IIA Series 1 37
   Mk IIA Series 2 37
   Mk IIB 39
   Mk IIB "Hurribomber" 39
   Mk IIC 41
   MK IID 44
   Official and unofficial Mk II Variations 44
   Mk III 46
   Mk IV 46
   Sea Hurricane 58
   Mk IA (Catafighter) 58
   Mk IB 59
   Mk IC 60
   Mk IIC 60
   Mk XII 60
   Licence-built versions 63
   Belgium 63
   Avions Fairey (Societé Anonyme Belge) Hurricane 63
   Yugoslavia 63
   Ikarus "Hurrischmitt" 63
   Persia 64
   Persian trainers 64
   Soviet Union 64
   Canada 66
   Experimental versions & designs 68
   Cancelled production types 68
   Hurricane Mk I – Technical Description 70
In Detail 76
   Fuselage 76
   Canopy 88
   Cockpit 92
   Wing 101
   Engine 112
   Tail 127
   Undercarriage 133
   Armament 141
Survivors 149

Acknowledgements

The author and publisher would like to thank: Mike Berry, Gary R Brown, Alex Crawford, Robert Gretzyngier, Dariusz Karnas, James Kightly, Tomasz Kopański, Martti Kujansuu, P. Lazel, Rob Leigh, Niall McWilliams, Steve Patterson, Jiri Rajlich, Robin Rawle, Przemysław Skulski, Jan Vd Heuvel.

Title page: *Preserved Hawker Hurricane Z5140 of the Historic Aircraft Collection in flight. (Dariusz Karnas)*

Introduction

The Hawker Hurricane is one of the symbols of the Battle of Britain, in service in greater numbers than the excellent Supermarine Spitfire during that conflict. The Hurricane was the main defender of Britain in 1940.

The "father" of the aircraft was the talented designer Sydney Camm, born in 1893, who before joining Hawkers had worked for seven years in the Martinsyde aircraft factory. Before the conception of the legendary fighter, he designed a number of successful biplanes, culminating in the Hawker Hart and its variants, the Demon, Audax, Hardy, Osprey, Hartbees, Hind and Hector. All of these types had proved their worth in service and were well-liked by pilots in all of the many countries where they were used. The Hart family, and the beautiful Hawker Fury fighter, were the pinnacle of British biplane development.

The Hawker Fury epitomised the RAF in the thirties, and was a very successful interceptor fighter design. As late as 1936, Hawker's started production of the improved version of the Fury, the Mk II, although they had already been given orders for production of the Hurricane. The Fury was the end of a stage in the firm's history and the end of an era in fighter design. The open-cockpit biplane had reached the peak of its development – there was nothing to improve in the Fury's configuration, as it stood. The era of the monoplane was arriving.

It was becoming apparent that the monoplane configuration was the future of fighter design, though the industry in Britain was slow to adopt the new technology. The opponents of the monoplane layout argued that the configuration would limit manoeuvrability, which was regarded as a critical factor in combat. There were also reservations about enclosed cockpits, which – according to the pilots – made flying difficult. (On the other hand it was believed that combat above 300 mph (480 kph) would prevent any manoeuvring or dogfights, and would limit combat to short "slashing" attacks). Previous Air Ministry specifications had unintentionally discouraged early attempts at a monoplane fighter for the RAF – F.7/30 for example, which was won by the Gloster Gladiator, required a take-off and landing distance that was at best marginal for monoplanes of the day. Indeed, the RAF's first monoplane bomber, the Fairey Hendon, had flown in 1930. So it was with some enthusiasm that the Air Ministry greeted Camm's suggestion of a monoplane development of the Fury.

A more reactionary tendency in some parts of the Air Ministry manifested itself in the specification for the armament of this future fighter. A 1930s requirement that dated back to the Great War was that the pilot must have the guns within arm's reach, to be able to re-cock them in the case of a jam, which still occurred regularly in the 1930s. This prevented location of the machine guns in the wings – the guns had to be situated either in the upper decking or the sides of the fuselage. The real problem was that the Vickers machine guns used by the RAF tended to jam, and the decision was taken to find a reliable gun. The chosen successor was the US-designed Colt 0.30 in (7.62 mm). However, the British gun was not an exact copy of its American prototype. The British used .303 calibre (7.7mm) ammunition for a large number of weapons and there was also a large stockpile of .303 ammunition, so for these reasons the Birmingham Small Arms factory (BSA) produced the Colt Browning recalibrated to .303in. As a result, the same machine gun in American and in Commonwealth service had different calibres.

Finally, after lengthy disputes and discussions, Specification F.5/34 was created for a new monoplane fighter.

Sydney Camm, Hawker's greatest designer. (Stratus coll)

A Hawker Fury getting some attention. Bearing a family resemblance to the Hart and the later Hurricane, this was one of the 1930s most elegant fighters. (via Alex Crawford)

Fury Monoplane

As early as 1933 Sydney Camm had started work on a preliminary design, and it was presented in August of that year to representatives of the Technical Office of the Air Ministry. The aircraft was a low-wing monoplane with tapering unswept wings with rounded tips. The Air Ministry was promoting the Rolls-Royce Goshawk engine at the time, and this engine was thus chosen as the power unit for the new aircraft. The fuselage was to a great extent similar to the Fury's, and together with the tail surfaces was practically unchanged in look and configuration, although of new construction. A new feature was that the pilot's cockpit was covered with a two-part canopy consisting of a windscreen and an aft-sliding canopy. The landing gear was fixed and enclosed by spats.

The structure of the aircraft was a clear development of previous practice, in line with the firm's abilities and experience. In general the structure was of metal with fabric covering, except for the front fuselage, which was covered with detachable metal panels. The armament consisted of four .303in (7.7 mm) Vickers machine guns, two were situated in the fuselage sides in such way that the pilot could reach them. The other two machine guns were situated in the wings. The calculated maximum speed was 270 mph (435 kph). The aircraft was nicknamed the "Fury Monoplane" and at the beginning it was a private venture.

The Fury Monoplane nearly became just another promising unbuilt design. The economic crisis of the 1930s and the international situation forced the British government to take a tough approach. They spread the little business there was among a wide variety of firms, aiming to keep them in "seed form" to enable massive expansion in the event of war.

This policy had a negative effect on the quality of proposed designs, and as a result the aviation industry remained without state subsidies for only two years. In 1935 the Under Secretary of State for Air, Sir Philip Sassoon, presented a programme of increased orders rising from seven to eleven million pounds in the next year.

Meanwhile, the Hawker company's situation was relatively healthy, in spite of the parsimonious Government. Hawker's came from the Sopwith company, which thanks to a series of superb scouts had grown into one of the largest and most successful aircraft manufacturers of the First World War. Following the war, however, large orders were cancelled and Tom Sopwith liquidated the business in 1920. Shortly afterwards Sopwith, his engineer Fred Sigrist, and his test pilot Harry Hawker set up H.G Hawker Engineering, but until the success of the Hart series, the challenging economic situation in the 1920s and 1930s meant that every contract had to be fought for. The large Kingston factory had to be leased out and Hawker returned to the converted skating rink where Sopwith had built his first stick-and-canvas biplane. In 1933 however, the business had been transformed into a public company and renamed Hawker Aircraft Ltd, finally acknowledging the organisation's long term concentration on the manufacture of aircraft. Increases in the production base started in February 1934, when the Hawker Aircraft Company bought controlling shares in the Gloster Aircraft Company and rights to its plant, which was then the largest in the UK. A bonus was also acquiring Gloster's Brockworth airfield. The take-over of Gloster's was no bad thing for this latter company, which was still manufacturing Gauntlets and preparing itself for production of Gladiators.

In 1935 Hawker took over all shares of the Armstrong Siddeley Development Company Ltd. and formed another public corporation, the Hawker Siddeley Aircraft Company Ltd. As a result of mergers and agreements, what was established was a powerful corporation consisting – besides Hawker and Gloster – of Sir W. G. Armstrong Whitworth Aircraft Ltd., Armstrong Siddeley Motors Ltd., Air Service Training Ltd and Avro Ltd. Soon the group extended its range by acquisition of other companies: de Havilland, Blackburn, Folland and a few smaller businesses. In 1937 the rest of Hawker Aircraft shares remaining in foreign hands were bought, strengthening the group's position and increasing its capital up to £6,000,000, making the organisation one of the most powerful players in the aircraft industry in the UK in those years.

In December 1933, the design of Camm's new fighter aroused interest in the Air Ministry, and at the same time a very promising engine from the Rolls-Royce stable called the PV (Private Venture) 12 (or XII) appeared, with the prototypes being tested in Derby. The new motor was a high-power twelve-cylinder "V" liquid-cooled in-line engine. The tests proceeded without significant problems and preliminary designers' calculations were realised. In July 1933, during a 100 hr test, the engine was measured attaining a take-off power of

K5083 at a very early stage, with fuselage machine guns. (Hawker Aircraft Ltd. via James Kightly)

635 hp (474 kW), and 800 hp (597 kW) at 12,140 ft (3,700 m). Obviously, however, it was still a long way to the beginning of mass production of the power unit, but its designers promised to increase engine power to 1,000 HP (764 kW).

In May 1934, seventeen draughtsmen and designers of the Hawker experimental department started work on the new variant of the Fury Monoplane, this time to be powered by the PV 12 engine instead of the Goshawk (which had been dropped by Rolls-Royce, as the evaporative cooling system could not be made to work effectively). In the course of one month a 1/10 scale mock-up was built, which was then sent to the National Physical Laboratory in Teddington for wind tunnel tests. The aircraft, which differed significantly from the original conception, was known as the Interceptor Monoplane. The armament consisted of four machine guns and the take-off weight amounted to 4,630 lb (2,100 kg). The cockpit was covered with a rearward-sliding canopy and the landing gear retracted into the wings. At an engine power of 1,014 hp (746 kW) the maximum speed was expected to reach 350 mph (563 kph).

The Air Ministry had issued the previously mentioned specification 5/34 – based partially on Camm's design assumptions – which was not yet a comprehensive set of requirements for the new fighter, but only a list of preliminary premises. The request was not for a prototype aircraft, but only the drawings and estimated performance data. Among postulated parameters was a maximum speed of 300 mph (480 kph) and the armament now to consist of four or six machine guns. The full set of requirements collected, in the form of a suitable specification, was intended to be issued at the end of 1934. Camm and his team had finished work on the design in August of that year and the documentation was handed over to the relevant Ministry department. As early as September 4th, 1934, the Air Ministry sent to Hawkers the requirement F.36/34, which in principle matched Camm's proposals. In fact it was just a clerical confirmation of the existing assumptions and not a new study worked out by Ministry experts. A letter enclosed detailed specifications and contained the requirement that Hawkers should present the mock-up of the new aircraft as soon as possible, which was defined simply as the "F.36/34 Single Seat Fighter". Camm fulfilled the task within the next two months and on February 21st, 1935, the factory received an official order (Contract No. 357483/34) for the manufacture of a new aircraft, which now was designated as the "High Speed Monoplane". The prototype was issued with the RAF serial number K5083. Its expected top speed was 320 mph (515 kph) at 15,000 ft (4,570 m).

The intended power unit for the High Speed Monoplane was the Rolls-Royce PV 12 engine, which was almost ready for production. Shortly thereafter, the engine was officially named the "Merlin", in keeping with Rolls-Royce's engines being named after birds of prey. The Rolls-Royce Merlin turned out to be one of the greatest aero-engines of all time, and it went on to be critical in the wartime success of not only Hurricanes, but also Spitfires, Mosquitoes, Lancasters and Mustangs, eventually powering over forty distinct types.

The armament of K5083 in specification F.36/34 was set according to Camm's design, i.e. two Vickers machine guns in the wing roots and two in the fuselage sides. However, when work on the prototype started, such a solution was seen as archaic and the fire power potentially too weak to knock down bombers in the brief firing opportunities likely to occur in the anticipated combats. Squadron Leader Ralph Sorley of the Air Ministry Armament Research Establishment, who was in charge of the Operational Requirements department, provided Camm semi-officially with details of research on the American 0.3 (7.62 mm) Colt MG-40 machine guns, which were proposed to be the standard RAF armament after their re-calibration to .303 (7.7 mm). Official, confirmed data was handed over to Hawkers on July 20th, 1935. The Browning machine guns (Colt MG-40 being the commercial name for what was modified into the British Browning) turned out to be relatively lightweight and very reliable, which enabled an installation of a greater number of guns per aircraft and removed the previously vital necessity of the pilot's immediate access to their breeches to clear stoppages or jams.

Camm regarded the wings as the best place for armament installation. According to his idea the outer wings should be fitted with four machine guns each, situated in a "box" between spars. This solution enabled easy access to the guns for ground crew. An additional advantage was the fact that the guns fired outside the airscrew disc, which saved weight on synchronisation and simplified the structure of the trigger mechanisms, as well as avoiding any reduction in the rate of fire.

The Ministry accepted Camm and Sorley's arguments, but was concerned that fabric-covered wings might not bear the recoil of such powerful armament. They ordered installation of wings of all-metal structure and skin. Camm was seriously worried about this requirement, because it could delay work on the prototype and besides, the all-metal wings were heavier, which would degrade the aircraft's performance. Additionally, the designer was convinced that Ministry experts' concerns were groundless and that wing strength calculations proved that even such a powerful battery of installed guns would not affect the wing's integrity. A compromise was agreed: Camm would start work on an all-metal wing, but the prototype and first experimental machines would be fitted with fabric-covered wings. Even the fabric-covered wings displayed a degree of innovation. Traditionally, canvas was stitched to the wing structure, but at the anticipated speeds the waxed string used for stitching would not be strong enough. The solution was to let a channel into each rib, into which the canvas was forced by a corresponding metal plate clamped to the rib. This assembly was smoothed over with a fabric tape, also reducing drag compared to traditional stitched wings. The prototype would not be armed, but would be fitted with suitable ballast. Meanwhile research into the strength of the wings would be conducted on the ground. Thanks to this, if the tests gave a positive result, it would be possible to start production of the aircraft, and – when the new wing was ready – to continue production according to Air Ministry guidelines

Hurricane Prototype K5083

Testing of the airframe and systems of the prototype K5083 started in August 1935, but the engine was still unavailable. Finally, one of the first Merlin C engines (No. 11) reached Hawker's Canbury Park Road workshop and was installed in the fighter's fuselage together with a two-blade wooden Watts Z33 airscrew of 11 ft 6 in (3.5 m) diameter. On October 23rd the disassembled prototype was transported from the Canbury Park Road workshops to Brooklands, where the aircraft was finally assembled and balanced; then the engine was tested on the ground. The last ground tests and pre-flight trials of prototype K5083 were finished at the beginning of November 1935, and on 6th of this month the 5,424 lb (2,460 kg) aircraft was test flown by Flight Lieutenant P. W. S. "George" Bulman, the head of the Hawker experimental pilot team.

K5083 was a single-seat, single-engine low-wing monoplane of mixed structure, with an enclosed cockpit and retractable landing gear. The fuselage structure was of Warren-truss construction, a framework of triangulated steel tubes made up of flat sections. This was covered with a light wooden frame itself covered with fabric, excepting the nose which was covered with metal panels. The cockpit was enclosed by a two-piece canopy, consisting of a windscreen and surrounds, and a rear-sliding cover. The wing centre-section was fitted with landing gear bays and fuel tanks, and the outer wings were fitted with mountings for eight .303" (7.7 mm) Browning Mk I machine guns. The prototype was unarmed, but guns were substituted with ballast of the same weight. The wing's extra lift devices consisted only of two-segment split flaps. The wing structure was similar to that of the fuselage, a metal frame made of spars and ribs covered with fabric, except the centre-section which was skinned with metal. The vertical tail unit with rudder and horizontal tail unit with elevators were similar structures. The horizontal tail was (initially) supported with struts, put in place due to concerns about potential flutter.

The main landing gear was retracted inwards by hydraulic power into the centre section. When retracted, the undercarriage was completely covered, and the doors fastened to the wheel legs were fitted with hinge-mounted flaps covering the lower part of the wheels. The tailwheel and pilot's footstep were retracted into the fuselage at the same time as the main gear.

The power unit consisted of a RR Merlin C engine (PV 12) of maximum power 1,025 hp (764 kW) at 11,000 ft (3,350 m). The fuel tanks had a total capacity of 107.60 gal (489l). The straight short exhaust pipes protruded slightly through oval holes in the engine cowling. The engine drove a two-blade fixed-pitch wooden Watts Z33 airscrew of 11 ft 6 in (3.505 m) diameter. The use of this type of airscrew was due to Air Ministry suspicion of the reliability of the newer propeller types. Although metal variable-pitch airscrews were commonly available in the USA, they were not in the UK or Europe.

K5083 spent a good part of its life on the ground. In January 1936 the Merlin C engine (No. 11) failed and was replaced with Merlin C No.15. At this point, some minor modifications were introduced to the airframe, especially to the canopy and radiator. The airscrew was replaced to test different types, several of which

The prototype Hawker Hurricane seen at the SBAC show at de Havilland's airfield Hatfield. (Paddy Heffernan, RAAF Museum via James Kightly)

The prototype Hurricane as rolled out at Brooklands, Surrey, showing the initial configuration and details. (via author)

were simply not suitable. Usually the aircraft flew with a two-blade Watts Z38 airscrew of 11 ft 3 in (3.4 m). diameter. In this configuration the prototype returned to test flying, and on February 7th, 1936 achieved a maximum speed of 315 mph (507 kph) at 16,200 ft (4,940 m) and weight of 5,670 lb (2,572 kg). The minimum speed was 57 mph (91 kph) in clean configuration.

On February 18th the aircraft was transferred to the Aeroplane and Armament Experimental Establishment (A&AEE) at Martlesham Heath for official flight tests preceding the order for production. The prototype was flown mainly by Bulman and Philip Lucas from Hawkers, and Sgt "Sammy" Wroath, one of the outstanding British pilots of the period. On March 16th, 1936 "Sammy" Wroath made the first flight after transfer to the A&AEE.

Another photograph from RAAF exchange officer Paddy Heffernan's album of the prototype Hurricane K5083 at the SBAC display. (Paddy Heffernan, RAAF Museum via James Kightly)

The prototype did not improve on its previous performance, and the maximum speed achieved at 14,600 ft (4450 m) was 315 mph (507 kph).

All test were finished by the beginning of 1937, but the prototype flew on, as the first production aircraft were held up waiting for an improved version of the Merlin engine. K5083 was then used in the movie "Test Pilot" starring Clark Gable. Of course Clark Gable did not fly any of the aircraft shown on the screen, the in-flight scenes were flown by "Sammy" Wroath. As early as July of 1935 K5083, flown by Wroath, was presented publicly during the RAF air display at Hendon.

In the meantime K5083 was modified. The sliding canopy, which was stiffened with a single vertical frame halfway along, turned out to be too flexible, jammed in its guides and resonated with in-flight vibrations, so it was strengthened. This was still not satisfactory, so two side frames were tried, then three. Finally, two vertical frames per side were adopted and that became the production canopy design. The radiator "bathtub" was lengthened to improve the airflow through the radiator, and the centre section of the flaps, which obstructed the radiator's efflux, was removed.

The main landing gear covers were modified and the lower outward folding flaps covering the wheels were removed. The struts supporting the horizontal tailplane were also removed, as flutter had not proved to be a problem.

In August 1936 a T.R.9B transceiver was installed with a wire antenna and mast, and the preferred armament set, consisting of eight .303in Browning machine guns, was fitted in the wings. During test flights the aircraft reached a speed of 318 mph (512 kph).

The Merlin C engine was replaced twice more, the first time with engine No. 17, when No. 15 engine failed, and the second time with No. 19, when No. 17 also failed. Problems with the "C" type Merlin caused it to be dropped as the proposed engine for the production aircraft, which had to wait for an improved version.

At the beginning of the war the prototype, stationed at Brooklands, was struck off the RAF roster. Nevertheless, T. P. Fiztgerald – the Hawker experimental pilot – reportedly flew a few combat flights against German bombers raiding the home airfield. There are also reports that during one of those flights he shot down an intruder. However, such reports should be treated sceptically. Probably the aircraft was used as a training machine for ground personnel, as it became instructional airframe 1211M in 1939. Some sources state that during its service the aircraft was fitted with a Merlin III engine.

Another photo of the prototype, 1935. (Stratus coll.)

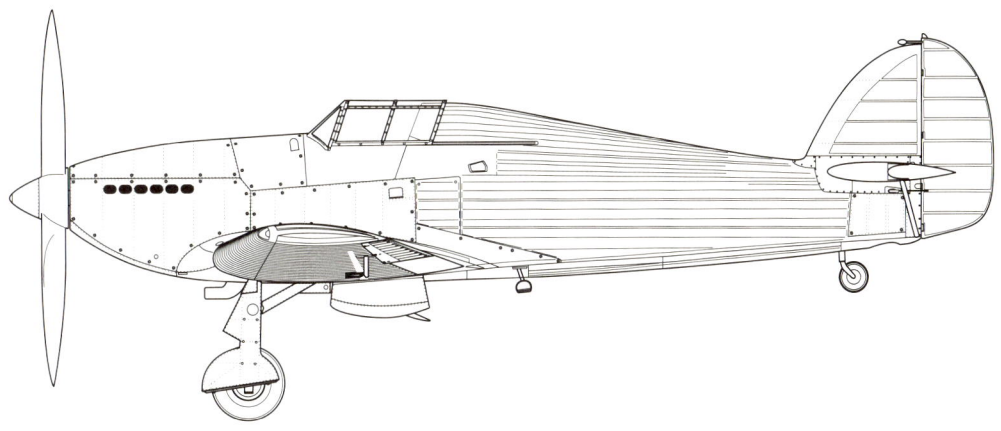

Hurricane prototype in its initial form.
1/72 scale.

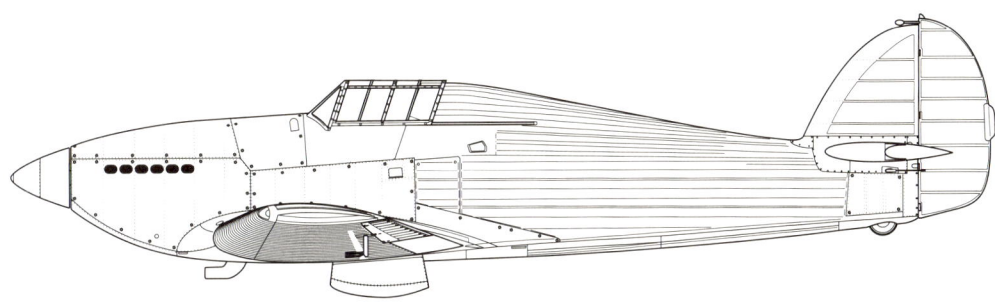

Hurricane prototype with modified canopy.
1/72 scale.

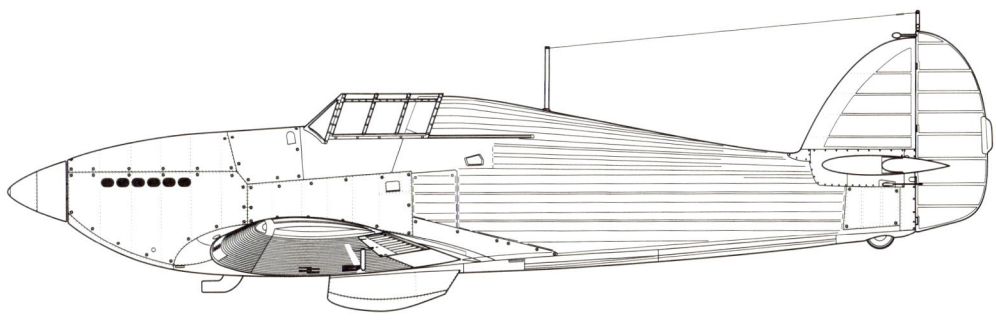

Hurricane prototype in final form.
1/72 scale

Versions

The Hurricane never went through the number of marks and versions that many other contemporary fighters did. All Hurricanes from the prototype on had the same fuselage construction, differing in detail but not structure, while the wing, initially fabric covered, was redesigned as a metal structure, but the planform and airfoil remained the same. Nevertheless, there were a significant number of versions of the Hurricane, some field modifications only undertaken in small numbers. The following data describes all known variants, including many never endorsed or produced by Hawkers themselves, as well as the main mark numbers. Versions which were not official Hawker or RAF marks are given in quotes.

Mk I

As early as April 1936 (or – according to some sources – in March) when K5083 was still undergoing testing, Hawkers decided to prepare a production line and jigs for the manufacture of 1,000 production aircraft at the Kingston and Brooklands factories.

On June 3rd, 1936, the Air Ministry gave the company order No. 5217112/36 for 600 fighters. In the UK, this was the greatest contract for a single type in the interwar period.

On June 26th, 1936, the Air Ministry issued the name for the new type – it was to be known as the "Hurricane". Unfortunately, however, production had not started because of the failure of the Merlin C engine (or Merlin Mk I) as a power unit for Hurricanes and Supermarine Spitfires. The new power unit was the improved Rolls-Royce Merlin G, which entered production as the Merlin Mk II. It was an engine of 890 hp (645 kW) take-off power at sea level at 2,850 rpm, and 1,030 hp (757 kW) at 16,000 ft (5,000 m) and 3,000 rpm.

The engine change caused almost a six-month delay to the schedule. It was necessary to redesign part of the fuel and cooling systems, and the engine mount itself. This was noticeable externally by the different shapes of the engine cowling panels. To enable preparation of the jigs and dies for the production line, one of first Merlins II (No. 7) was sent to the Kingston plant. The same engine was installed in the first production Hawker Hurricane fighter (L1547, production order No. 3002), which left the factory on April 19th, 1937.

Ground tests of this machine lasted until October. As late as October 12th, at Brooklands, the aircraft made its first flight flown by P.G. Lucas. The fighter weighed 5,460 lb (2,476 kg). During the next month, six more Hurricane Mk I aircraft were test flown (according to some sources four more) against production order No.3010, which allocated Hurricanes serial numbers L1548 to L1597.

The basic difference from the prototype was the new Merlin III engine in production aircraft, with a two-blade fixed-pitch Watts Z38 airscrew of 11 ft 3 in (3.4m) diameter. The initial three-segment exhaust pipe unit is normally referred to as the "kidney style exhaust".

The first production Hurricane L1547. (P. Lazell coll.)

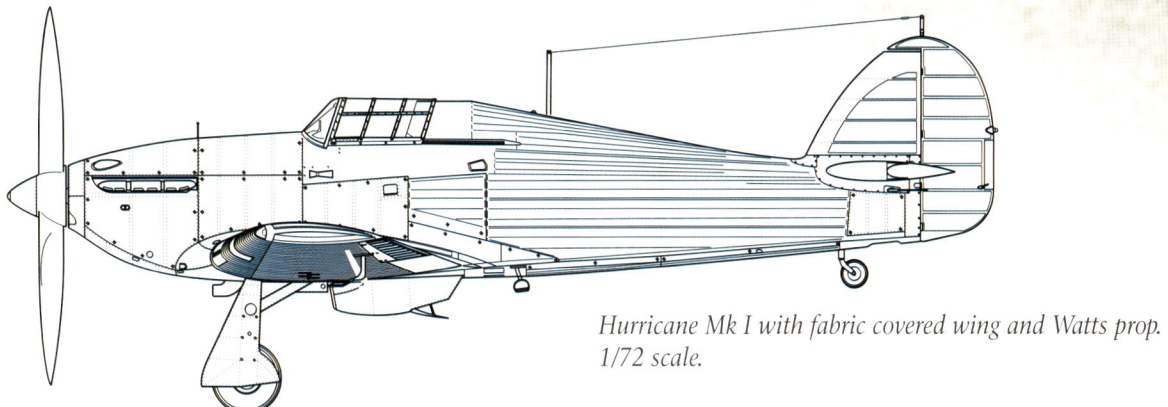

Hurricane Mk I with fabric covered wing and Watts prop. 1/72 scale.

The carburettor intake under the fuselage was shortened. On the port fuselage side under the windscreen, a venturi tube for the instruments was installed. The fuselage spine behind the pilot's cockpit was flattened out, forming the characteristic "broken" line to the Hurricane's upper profile, because the smooth curved spine complicated production. The main landing gear doors were also modified, and consisted of two pieces, the main unit covering the wheel leg and half of the wheel and a small flap at the top of the leg covering its attachment point. It is certain that the first Hurricane, L1547, had this set-up, and quite probably other early machines as well. The small flaps were complicated and were soon removed, leaving a noticeable gap with the undercarriage up. Later aircraft had single-piece doors, which had a distinctive wedge shape section to assist emergency lowering through their aerodynamic effect.

Other than those details, the first Hurricanes were identical to the prototype in its final form. Fuel tanks were situated under the pilot's seat and in the wing centre section, while the outer wings contained the gun bays. Each wing contained four .303 Colt/Browning machine guns with 334 rounds per gun. The harmonisation was set to 2,000 ft (595 m). In September 1939 this was changed to 400 yards (365 m) and in May 1940 to 200 yards (183 m), although expert pilots set their own fire patterns.

The first unit equipped with the new fighters was 111 Squadron, known as "Treble One", commanded by Squadron Leader John Gillan and stationed at Northolt. The first four Hurricanes were delivered just before Christmas 1937. By February 1938 the squadron had 16 machines.

The production rate of Hurricanes was now so swift that squadrons were unable to keep up with deliveries. The next squadrons (3 and 56) were re-equipped with the new type, but in the first half of 1938 only 50 aircraft from the total of 80 built were delivered to RAF units. However, these machines also differed from the first ones.

Even while the first batches of the new fighters were leaving the production lines in Kingston and Brooklands, Camm and his team were still "tweaking" the design, and introducing a series of modifications. Some confusion is caused by the fact that some of the earliest produced Hurricanes had the later modifications added, meaning that they look like late production aircraft.

Early Mk I Hurricanes, probably of 85 Sqn, being presented to the press. Note the two colour fuselage roundels. (Robert Gretzyngier)

11

Early Hurricanes were fitted with a plain glazed windscreen. When armoured glass became a requirement, initially a sheet was fixed on externally, but not as an integral part of the windscreen structure. To make it integral required significant changes to the canopy frame. The first aircraft fitted with the experimental new windscreen was L1750. An additional feature was an armoured plate behind the pilot's head, which was trialled on L1562. Seat armour did not become a standard fitting until after the Battle of France. Some of last Hurricanes with two-blade airscrews and fabric-covered wings were fitted with a windscreen-mounted rear-view mirror, which slightly improved the visibility rearwards, which was otherwise regarded as poor, but pre-war had not been thought of as important.

Right: *Another view of the brand new early series Hurricane Mk Is of 111 Sqn, at RAF Northolt.*

Below: *His Majesty King George VI (top, centre) is shown over an early production Hurricane of 111 Sqn. The fabric wing gun bay hatches and structure is clearly shown (both Robert Gretzyngier)*

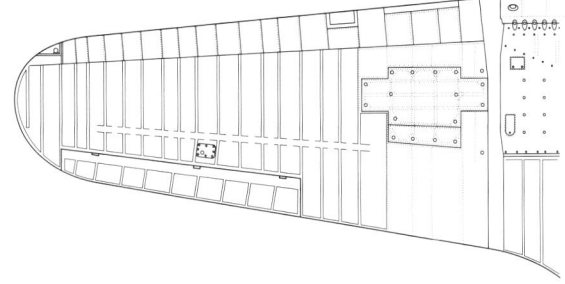
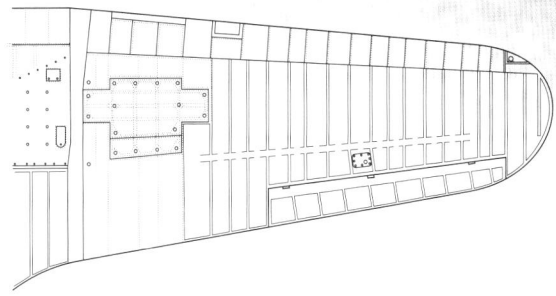

Wooden wings. 1/72 scale.

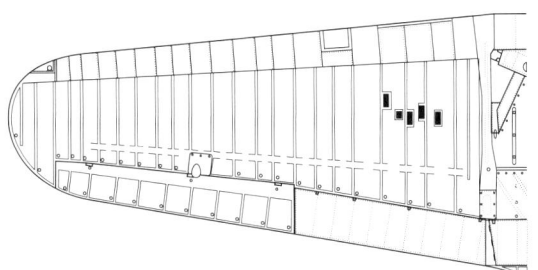
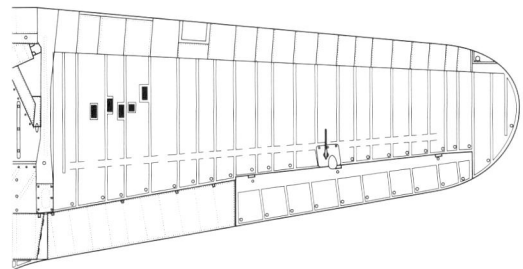

The venturi tube was replaced by a pitot tube. The exhaust pipes were also changed. Grouped into cylinder exhaust pairs, the holes of the first two units were crescent-shaped, and the third round. These were known as "ejector exhausts" as, by diverting the gases aft, they added to the engine's thrust.

Because the tailwheel often jammed in the retracted position, leading to fuselage damage during the subsequent landing, in front-line squadrons it was usually locked down. Most early Hurricanes were modified to this standard during overhauls and factory inspections.

The most important modification introduced at this stage of the Hurricane's development was the installation of a ventral fin under the rear fuselage. This modification was the result of spin performance concerns, with tests performed at the end of 1937 at the A&AEE and the National Physics Laboratory wind-tunnel at the suggestion of "George" Bullman. The tests proved the necessity of increasing the rudder area by lengthening it by 6 in (15 cm) downwards. To avoid redesigning the whole rear fuselage, it was decided to introduce a long ventral fin aerodynamically leading in to the new lower part of the rudder. This smoothed the airflow over the lower fuselage, and improved spin recovery and lateral control in the landing phase. Simultaneously with the implementation of this modification in March 1938, on production aircraft (only 50 aircraft had been manufactured), it was decided to install a fixed tailwheel with a lengthened leg, accepting this as a sensible solution to the retraction problems.

The aircraft quickly became popular with the RAF pilots. It was manoeuvrable, fast and responsive in the air. It behaved excellently on rough grass airfields thanks to the wide wheel track. Later, when obliged to use airfields with runways, the Hurricane proved to be relatively tolerant of crosswinds, which significantly improved the ease of take-off and landing. In this respect the Hurricane was better then the Spitfire, which had a much narrower undercarriage track and thus was more difficult to manage while taxiing.

The groundcrews' experience of the Hurricane was also positive. Despite being a significant step forward in technology and thus complexity, it was relatively easy to maintain, even for less experienced fitters and riggers. Due to the number of access panels, access to components such as the engine was easy. As soon as the Hurricane was used in combat, it became evident that it had a very tough structure which allowed it to return to base with significant damage. Then repair was relatively straightforward even under field conditions. The ease of repair and rebuild of the type was also demonstrated by the fact that repair units scattered throughout the country fixed 4,537 damaged Hurricanes.

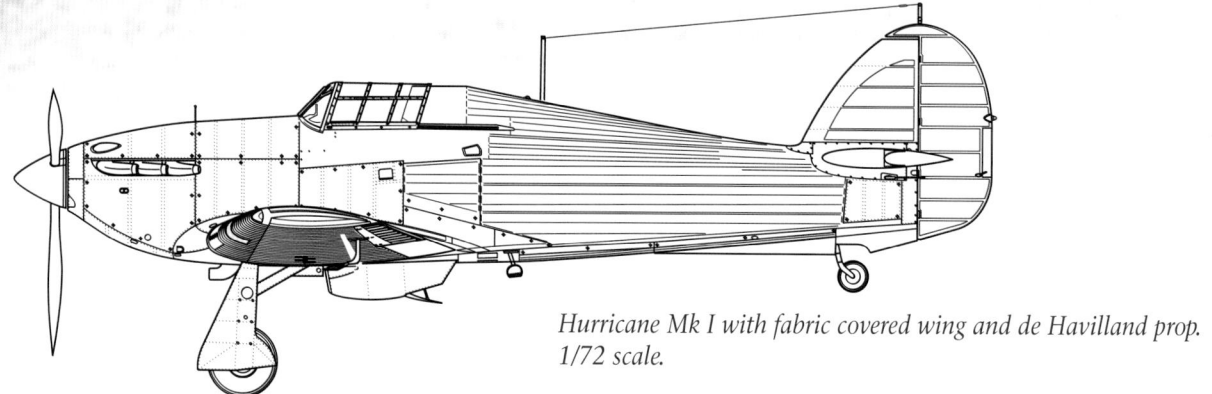

Hurricane Mk I with fabric covered wing and de Havilland prop. 1/72 scale.

Hurricane L1586 seen at Church Fenton some time in 1938. This aircraft served with both 73 and 79 Sqns during 1938. Early production Mk I with an interesting variation on the "Night/White" undersides. Only the outer wing panels are painted Night & White, with the centre section and fuselage undersides in Aluminium.
Bottom: Hurricane P2798/LK•A of 87 Sqn. This was the personal aircraft of Flt Lt Ian Gleed, OC A Flt and carried the "Figaro" cartoon cat on the starboard side of the cockpit. Note the large Rotol spinner, oversize fuselage roundels and codes, and the glare shield and rear view mirror fitted to LK•A. *(all photos C. Goss collection)*

Mk I (late series)

The main obstacle preventing the use of the full potential of the airframe and engine combination was the two-blade fixed-pitch aircrew, which was, by necessity, a compromise between converting power at high speeds and low. In July 1938 it was decided to replace the Watts airscrew with a three-blade metal two-pitch Hamilton Standard airscrew of 11ft (3.352 m) diameter, which was license-produced by de Havilland under the designation 5/31 or 5/32. The total weight of the pitch adjustment gear, spinner and airscrew itself was greater than for the previous unit, but nevertheless it gave a speed increase of 17 mph (27 kph) and enabled better utilisation of engine power through the airscrew's changeable pitch. The de Havilland airscrew had only two pitch settings. In July 1938, L1562 (used previously for armoured headrest tests) was the first aircraft fitted with this airscrew.

In the autumn of 1938, Rotol (a company set up to produce propellers and airscrews by Rolls-Royce and Bristol) manufactured a three-blade hydraulically-adjustable R.X.5/2 airscrew of 10 ft 9 inch (3.277 m) diameter, with blades made of compressed wood and with fully variable pitch. Simultaneously Rolls-Royce had started manufacture of a new version of the Merlin engine, which differed by being able to use both Rotol and de Havilland airscrews (the Merlin II could only be fitted with Watts or de Havilland airscrews). The Merlin III was fitted with a modified oil system, which enabled pressurised oil to be used for airscrew pitch adjustment. The first Rotol airscrews were delivered to Hawker for tests on an experimental aircraft. This was Hurricane L1606 bought back from the RAF and registered to Hawkers as G-AFKX. The machine was fitted with the Merlin III serial No. 11111. (Some sources claim that the aircraft marked G-AFKX was the Hurricane L1877 or L2026 from 56 Sqn, which met with an accident and was subsequently repaired.) In any case G-AFKX remained with Hawker and was used for airscrew and engine tests, including, among others, the Merlin R.M.4.S and the Merlin 45. The first aircraft with the Merlin III engine flew on January 24th, 1939, with Lucas at the controls. The machine achieved a maximum speed of 344 mph (554 kph) at 15,000 ft (4,572 m).

The performance of the Rotol-equipped aircraft was significantly better than the earlier versions. The aircraft performed better during take-off and landing; it also had a greater climb rate, the level speed increased and a faster dive was possible. Practically all parameters were improved by use of the new airscrew. Nevertheless, the new propeller did not replaced the old types at once – for a period Hurricanes were manufactured with both new Rotol and older de Havilland propellers.

The old spinner was unsuitable, and the new one designed especially for the Hurricane was not yet ready. Because the Merlin III and Rotol propeller combination was also used by the Spitfire Mk I, it was decided to use the Spitfire spinner, which had only a slightly greater diameter. Later a special, longer, spinner designed especially for the Hurricane was brought on line.

Below are the performance details for the Hurricane when fitted with Watts and with Rotol airscrews (reliable data for the de Havilland airscrew is hard to find)

Hurricane Mk I	Watts airscrew engine Merlin II		Rotol airscrew engine Merlin III	
Max speed	318 mph	511 kph	328 mph	528 kph
Climb to 2,000 ft (6,100 m)	11.7 min		9.8 min	
Range	522 miles	840 km	502 miles	808 km
Ceiling	30,000 ft	9140 m	31,000 ft	9,450 m

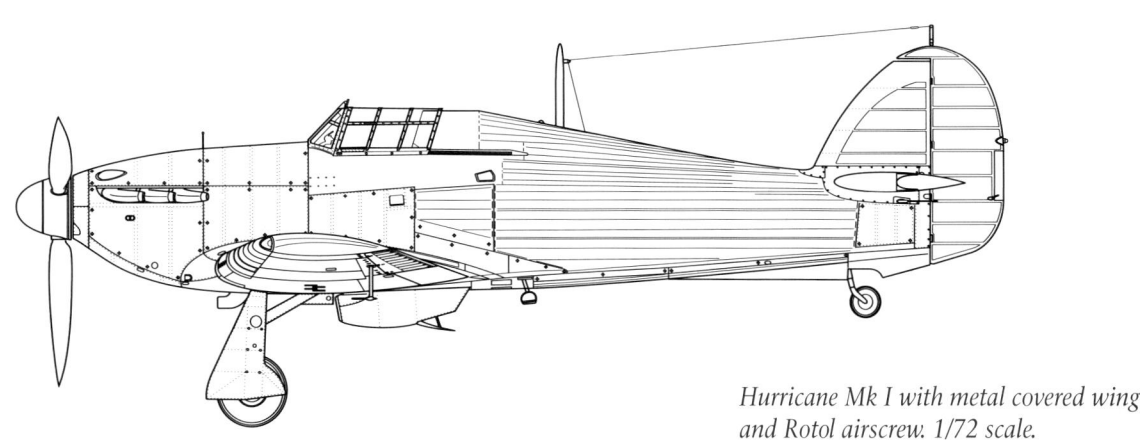

Hurricane Mk I with metal covered wing and Rotol airscrew. 1/72 scale.

The Rotol airscrew was the greatest modification to that date introduced on production Hurricane Mk I aircraft, but the all-metal wings were introduced almost simultaneously. In hindsight it is interesting that the designation of the aircraft was unchanged – it remained the Hurricane Mk I.

Work on the design of the metal wing was conducted at the same time as production was underway on the manufacture of fabric winged Hurricanes. In September 1939, L1887, the first aircraft with the new wings, flew. The shape of the gun-bay hatches changed – now it consisted of four segments instead of two. As the testing of L1887 was underway, the manufacture of new wings for the last machines from the first production order was commenced.

It is difficult to estimate how many Hurricanes were fitted with fabric-covered wings and how many with metal wings at the factory. It's possible 430 machines from the first production order were fitted with the fabric wings and the remaining 130 with new metal ones. However, during overhauls and inspections of Hurricanes in RAF service, the old wings were replaced with metal, but the exact number of aircraft modified in this way remains unknown.

Additional confusion about this question is caused by the fact that about eighty aircraft from the second and 25 from the third production orders were built during the fabric wing production period. How many of them (if any) were fitted with new wings is unknown.

Minor modifications (among others) comprised replacement of ring & bead gunsights with reflector ones (GM2 type), and the TR.9B radio transceivers were replaced with the TR.9D, and later, in 1940, with the TR.1133. The new windscreen with strengthened structure was installed, with armoured glass being an integral part of it. The rear-view mirror also became standard equipment.

Before the Kingston and Brooklands plants finished the first 600 production aircraft, on September 29th, 1939, the Hawker company received an order for next 300 machines. Manufacture of this batch was entrusted to the same factories, and the contract (No.751458/38) ordered production of aircraft only with Rotol airscrews and Merlin III engines. Just over one month later, in November 1939, the next 500 Hurricanes were ordered. Their production was to be at Gloster's factory in Brockworth, Gloucestershire, according to contract No.962371/38/C23A. The next order for 500 machines (plus 44 aircraft as a supplement for those lost) – contract No. 962371/38 – was again submitted to the Kingston, Brooklands and Langley plants.

The next 40 Hurricane Mk I aircraft were manufactured in Canada at the Canadian Car & Foundry Corporation plant in Montreal, Quebec. Their official designation was the Canadian Hurricane Mk I. The setting up of Canadian production of the Hurricane is an interesting story in its own right, which we cannot go into in detail here. Suffice it to say that after initial Air Ministry reluctance, pressure from the Canadians plus an offer of RCAF Squadrons in time of war enabled licence production to be undertaken.

Two photographs of wrecked Hurricanes overtaken by the German advances in Europe, May 1940. German souvenir hunters have already been at work. (Tomasz Kopański)

This was no small achievement, involving among other items 82,000 microfilmed drawings of all the tools and jigs and components being made and sent across the Atlantic.

In May 1940 the Gloster plant at Brockworth started delivery of the next 100 aircraft, against contract No. 19773/39/23a. Some 1,250 machines from the next order (No. 85730/40/23a) were built, some of them equipped with the de Havilland airscrew. The last order for the Hurricane Mk I was undertaken by the Langley plant (contract No. 62305/39). This order was for 500 machines with the Merlin III engine. Twenty-five of them had fabric-covered wings, but probably most of these were retrofitted, at the factory, with metal wings.

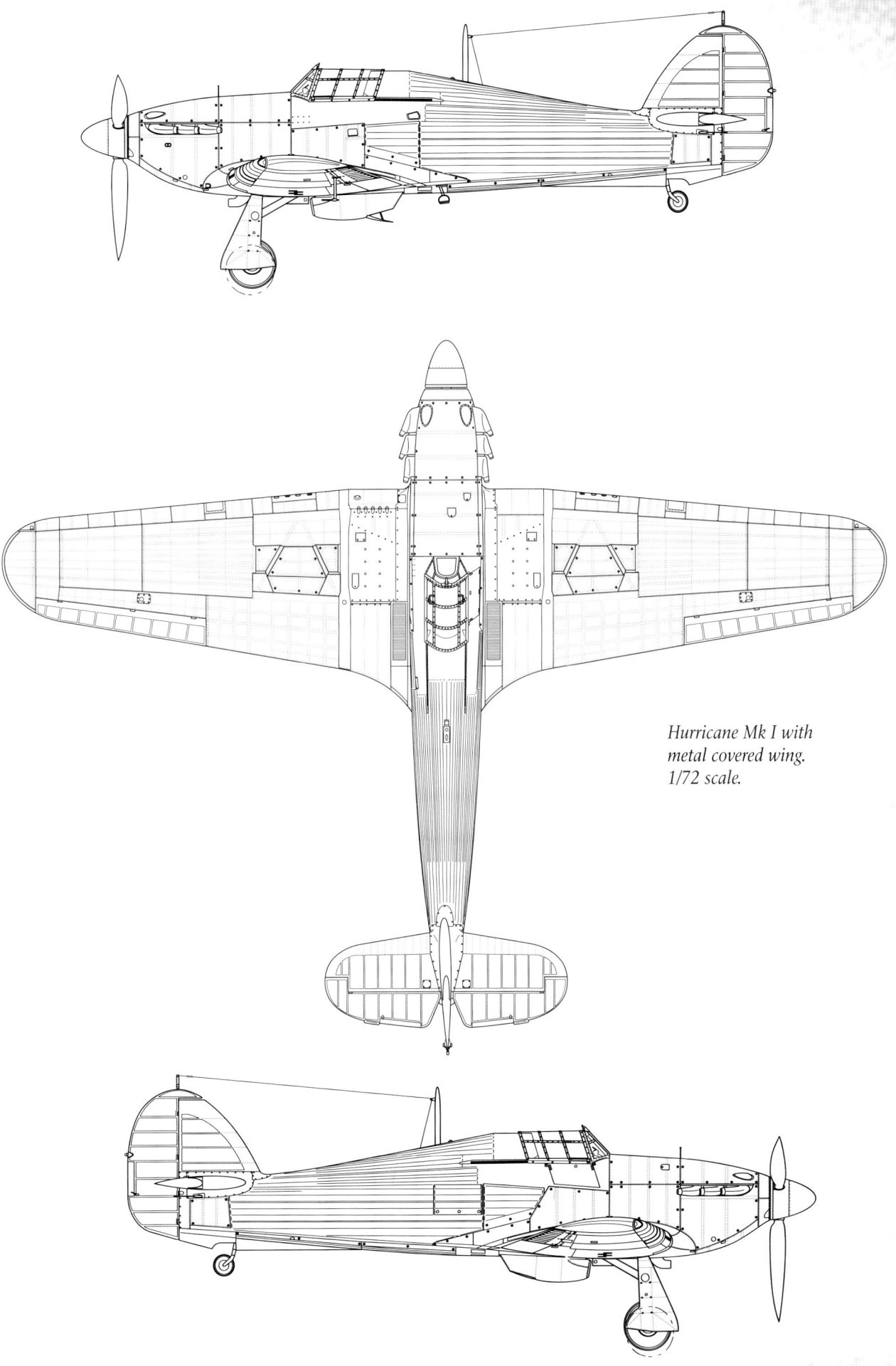

Hurricane Mk I with metal covered wing. 1/72 scale.

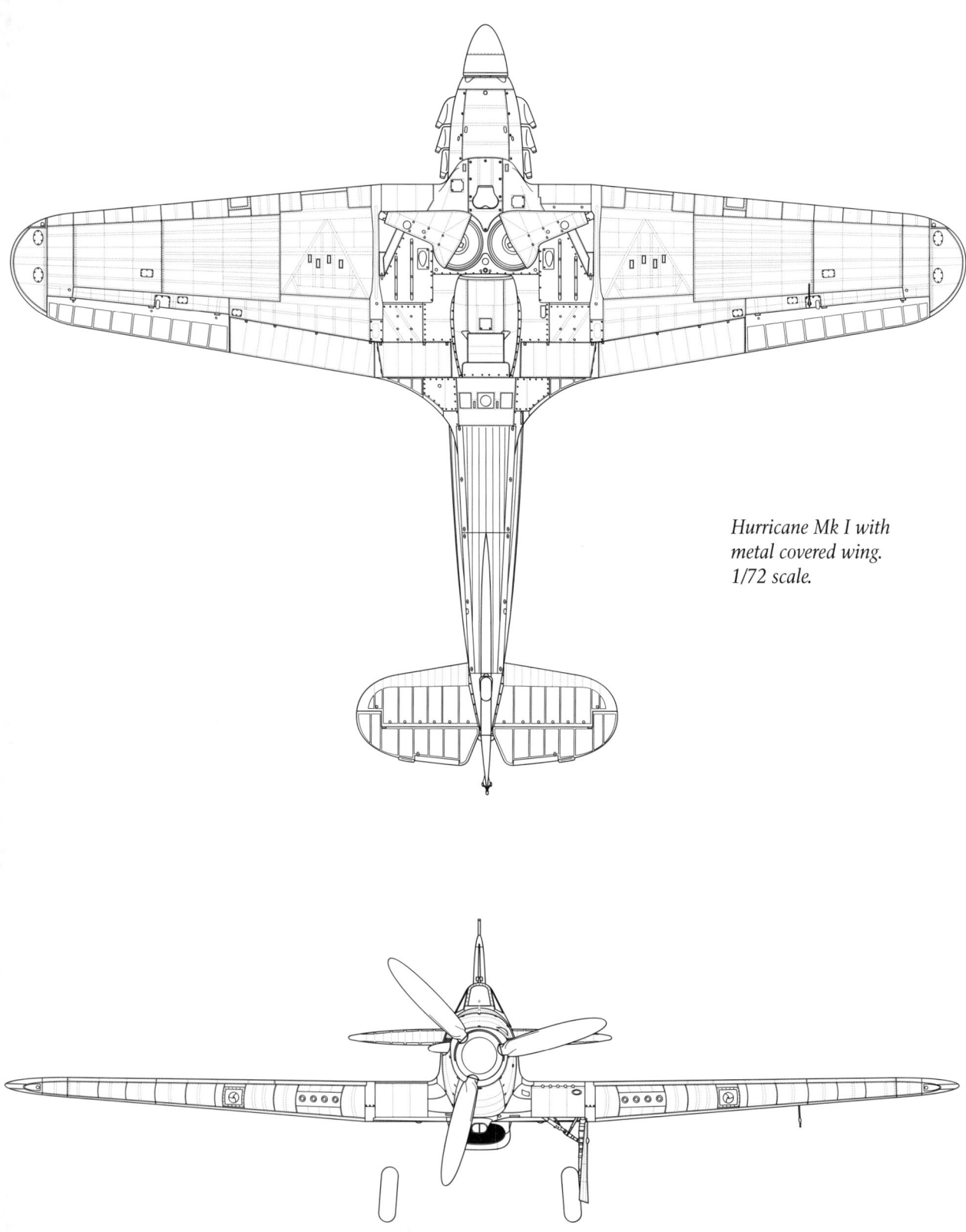

Hurricane Mk I with metal covered wing. 1/72 scale.

Official and unofficial Mk I Variations

Mk I (Trop)

As early as 1938 Hawker received an order for a fighter aircraft for Persia. It was decided that the aircraft would be an export version of the Hurricane, adapted to conditions prevailing in the client's country: high temperatures with dust and sand.

The major modification was installation of a Vokes dust filter with an Aero-Vee insert protecting the carburettor against sand. The filter together with its large housing was installed under the engine cowling on aircraft L1669 and L1893. Just behind the pilot's cockpit an additional water tank was installed. L1669 was first flown in July 1939 by the Hawker experimental pilot Dick Reynell. Soon after L1893 and L1877 were flown, the latter being fitted with a Rolls-Royce air filter.

Although the maximum speed dropped by almost 25 mph (40 kph), installation of the tropical filter did not cause a significant reduction in the other aspects of the aircraft's combat performance, as was at first feared.

As well as the tropical filter other modifications were introduced to adapt the aircraft to the anticipated conditions, such as cockpit ventilation (recognisable from the outside through two air inlets below the canopy) and a pilot's "survival kit" consisting of a gun, a mirror, an airtight water & food container, a woollen blanket, and a rifle (Lee-Enfield .303) for self-defence. Standard Hurricanes were converted to tropical specification in field workshops and repair units in the Middle East, and rarely in production.

Just after the outbreak of war Hurricane L1669 was sent to Khartoum for tropical trials. The resulting modifications were incorporated in later production machines of all versions. It is difficult to determine exactly how many Hurricane Mk Is were tropicalised, but they were mainly aircraft used in the Middle East and Mediterranean area.

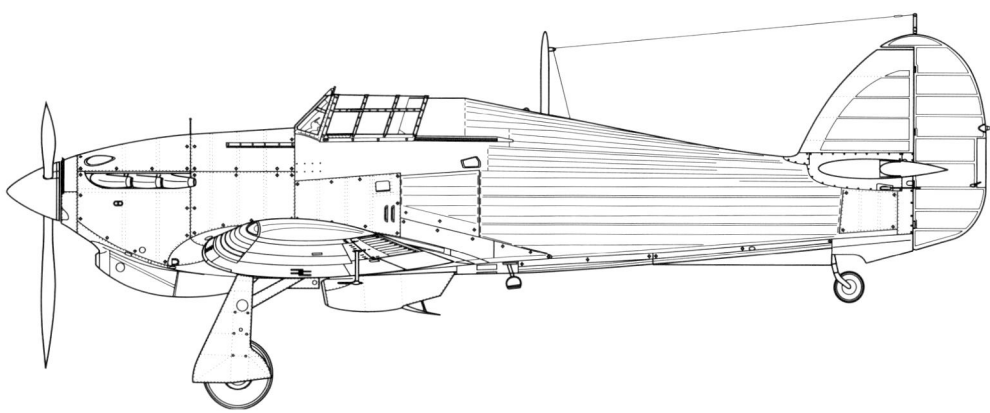

"Tac R. Mk I"

The first recorded use of the Hurricane for tactical reconnaissance took place in November – December 1940 with 208 Sqn stationed in the Western Desert in North Africa. The squadron previously used Westland Lysanders, but a faster machine would be much better in the reconnaissance role. For test purposes one tropicalised Hurricane Mk I (V7295) was fitted with a vertically mounted camera just behind the pilot's cockpit. After that, about eight (the exact number is uncertain) Hurricane Mk Is were reconfigured by 103 Maintenance Unit (MU) in the same way. Three of them were later used by 208 Sqn in Gambut (Libya) in February 1941. They flew in formation with Lysanders and standard Hurricane fighters, whose task was to escort the reconnaissance aircraft. When the squadron was transferred to Greece on April 1st, 1941, the reconnaissance Hurricanes (designated Tac R. Mk I) probably remained in North Africa. Two of them were stationed in Khartoum, one went to 73 Sqn, one to 1 South African Air Force (SAAF) Sqn and another one to 451 Sqn Royal Australian Air Force (RAAF). Single aircraft were also transferred to other units. Some of them were fitted with additional radio equipment enabling direct communication with ground troops, and thus could be used to direct artillery fire.

Long range Hurricane at Luqa, Malta. (P. Lazell)

Nosed-over Hurricane at Ta' Qali, Malta.

A Hurricane I (de Havilland prop) in North Africa, possibly of 3 Sqn SAAF, with an unusual colour scheme applied to the forward fuselage and wing leading edges. It has been suggested this scheme, seen on several of the unit's Hurricanes, was intended to mimic Italian camouflage and fool enemy AA gunners.

Another Mk I with de Havilland propeller, being refuelled in North Africa, 1940/41. (All P. Lazell collection)

"PR Mk I"

At the same time a similar conversion was undertaken at Helipolis in Egypt. This was inspired by the formation of 2 Photo Reconnaissance Unit (2 PRU) and the establishment of the Intelligence Photo Flight led by Squadron Leader Hugh McPhail in Cairo. Because the new unit could not get reconnaissance Spitfires, it was decided to adapt available Hurricanes for Photo Reconnaissance (PR) purposes. This led to creation of the PR Mk I version. This version could perform long-range flights at a height of 30,000ft (9,144 m). The first converted aircraft was DG613/G which, in May 1941 at Helipolis, was fitted with three 14in F.24 cameras behind pilot's cockpit, one of them installed vertically, the other two obliquely. (The "G" suffix to the serial indicated that the aircraft must be kept under guard at all times while on the ground). Another two aircraft (V7423 and V7428) were fitted with two 8in F.24 cameras. Their lenses protruded slightly from the fuselage, and thus were covered with a special fairing. The aircraft had some of the armament removed (perhaps all) and the guns were replaced with additional fuel tanks, which resulted in a total fuel capacity of **194 gal (882 l)**. The next aircraft of this version were built on Malta.

It is difficult to determine how many Mk Is were converted to reconnaissance aircraft – estimated numbers vary from a handful to about twenty. However, it is certain that they were equipped with various combinations of one, two or three cameras with different focal lengths. After the arrival of the latest German fighters to this theatre the remaining PR Hurricanes were transferred to India.

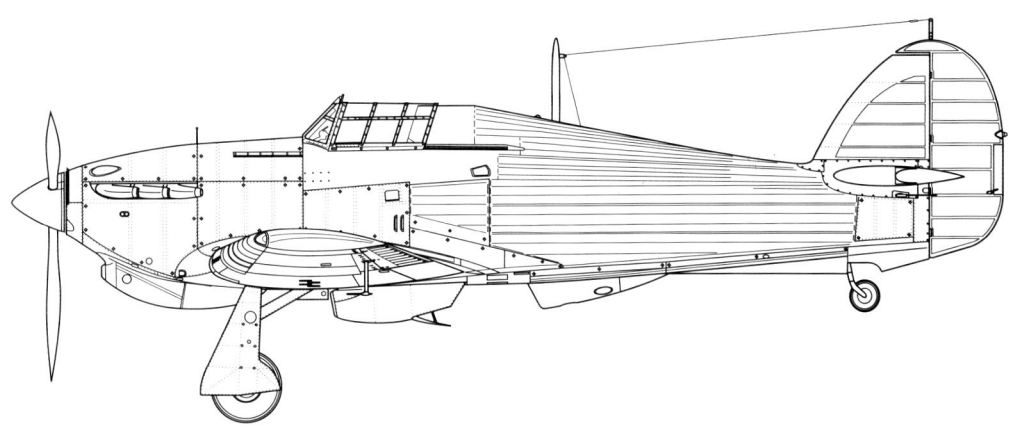

Hurricane PR Mk I 1/72 scale.

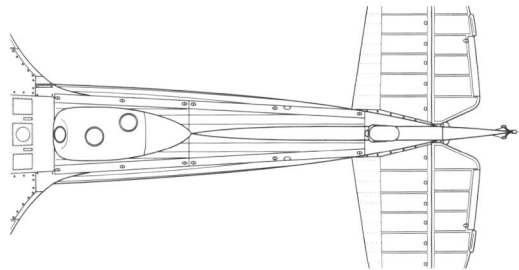

NF Mk I

Like all previous pre-war RAF aircraft, in the Air Ministry specification the Hurricane (and Spitfire) were expected to act as day and night fighters. However the art of night fighting and the complexity of the required equipment and higher speeds had not been accounted for by any combatants, until the need actually arose. It quickly became evident that night fighters and night fighter units were required to be different from day fighter types, crews and units. In the latter half of September 1940, the Germans, who had lost the fight for air superiority over England, intensified their night bomber offensive against British cities. Initially, this was quite successful, because the RAF had no dedicated night fighters able to operate in the dark against German raiders. Desperate efforts were made to adapt many types. This led to creation of the night fighter version of the Bristol Blenheim. Small numbers of Boulton Paul Defiants were also available.

Certain successes were also achieved during "Intruder" missions. The first such mission was flown by a 23 Sqn Blenheim in December 1940, and in January of the next year 87 Sqn with Hurricane Mk I aircraft started similar missions. The typical operational method was an ambush in the vicinity of airfields in France, from whence the raids against Britain started. When German bombers, perhaps damaged by anti-aircraft (AA) fire and with low fuel reserves, approached their bases for landing, the Hurricanes hidden in darkness attacked the bombers, which were often illuminated with their landing lights on.

After re-equipment with the Hurricane Mk IIC the effectiveness of the "intruders" grew significantly. An outstanding performer was Czech Flight Lieutenant K M. Kuttelwascher, who shot down 18 enemy aircraft. In just one night (May 2nd, 1942) over St. André he shot down three He 111s, only using five seconds' ammunition.

21

It seemed that the Hurricane was reasonably well suited to night missions, with a wide wheel track and relatively low landing speed it could more frequently take-off and return from a mission safely even with only a dimly-lit airfield than the Spitfire. However, in the case of the Mk I, its use was just a makeshift expedient, as the requirement for specialised night fighters was developed. The modifications were not very complicated and were limited to replacement of three-segment exhaust pipes with six individual ones and to installation of rectangular plates on the fuselage sides just in front of the windscreen, to shield the pilot's view of the bright exhaust flames.

The latter modification turned out to be so successful that similar shields were often installed on day-fighter Hurricanes. Night-operating Mk Is were very rare, and only with entry into service of the Mk II version did Hurricanes appear in significant numbers in this role. Night operational Hurricane Mk Is were not equipped with radar, and thus their operational abilities were significantly limited.

Another disadvantage of this version was relatively unsuitable armament. In a night combat there is rarely opportunity to fire long bursts. The target would appear just for a moment, and each manoeuvre could cause the hunter to lose visual contact with his prey. In such situations eight .303 guns were insufficient for shooting down an enemy aircraft, except by lucky chance if a bullet managed to hit vital parts of an aircraft or crew.

Hurricane night fighter, showing the six-stub exhaust and glare shield, with black overall camouflage. Personal mount of PO Kloboucnik, 96 Sqn, Cranage 1941 (Jiri Rajlich)

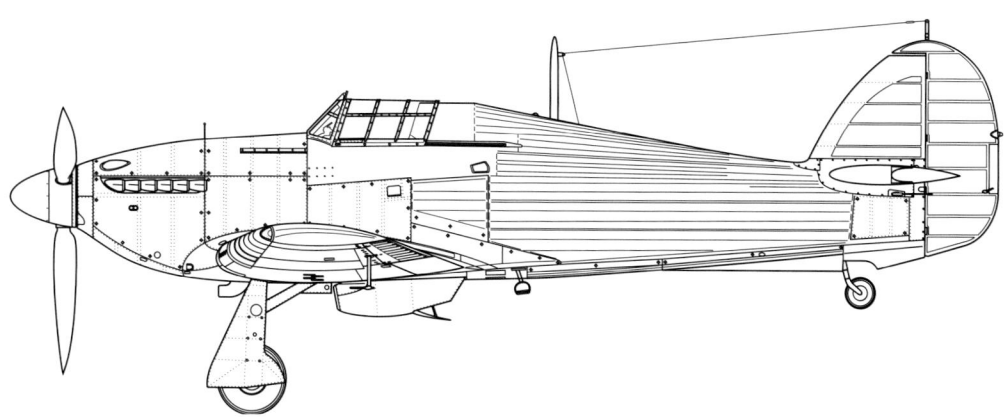

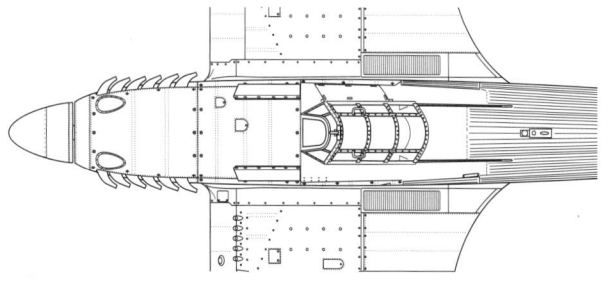

*Hurricane NF Mk I
1/72 scale.*

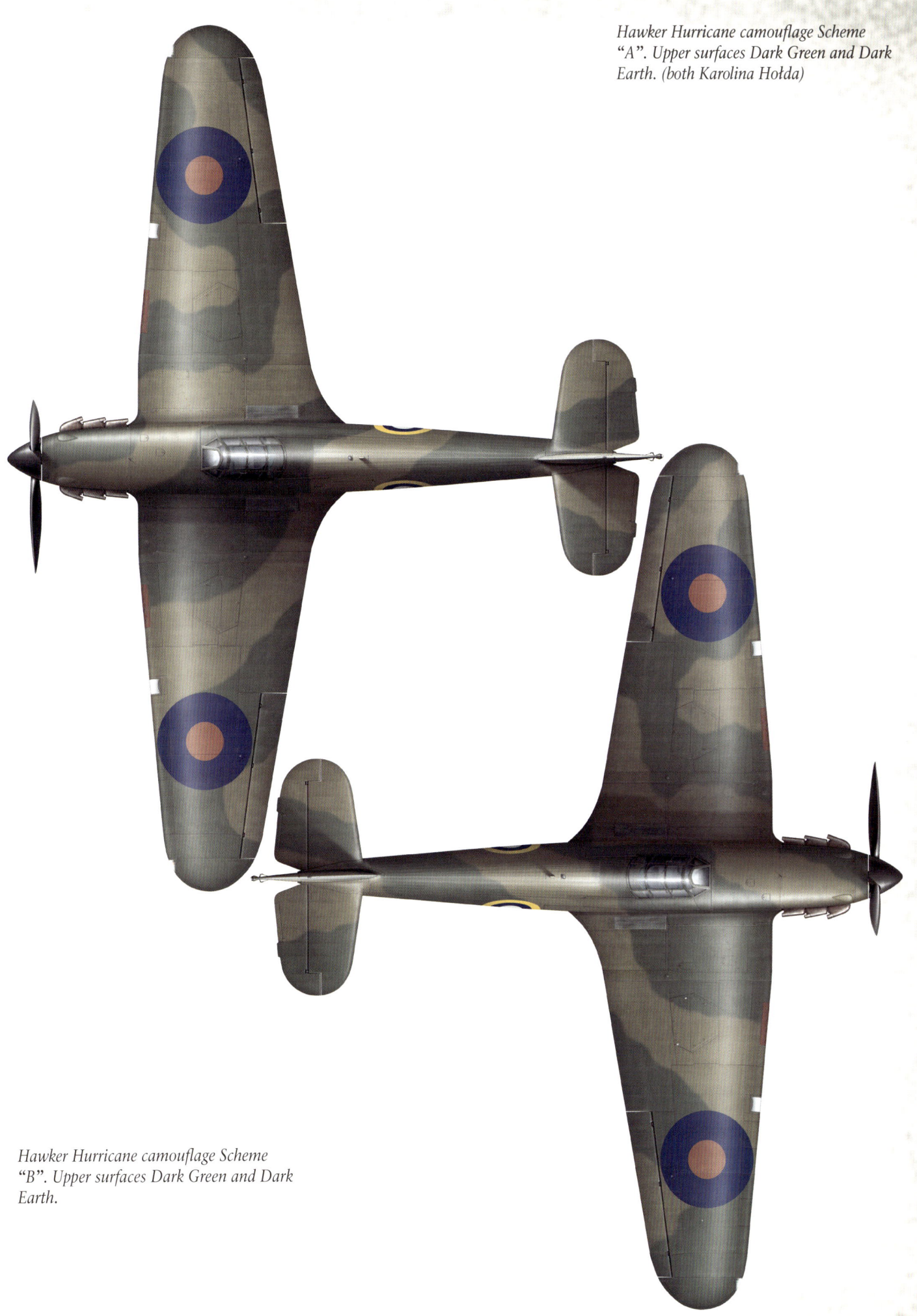

Hawker Hurricane camouflage Scheme "A". Upper surfaces Dark Green and Dark Earth. (both Karolina Hołda)

Hawker Hurricane camouflage Scheme "B". Upper surfaces Dark Green and Dark Earth.

Hurricane undersurfaces on initial production aircraft. Undersurfaces silver with black serial and three colours roundel.

B: Day-Night scheme. Undersurafes silver with Matt Black and Matt White outer wings. Black and white serials and three colours roundel.

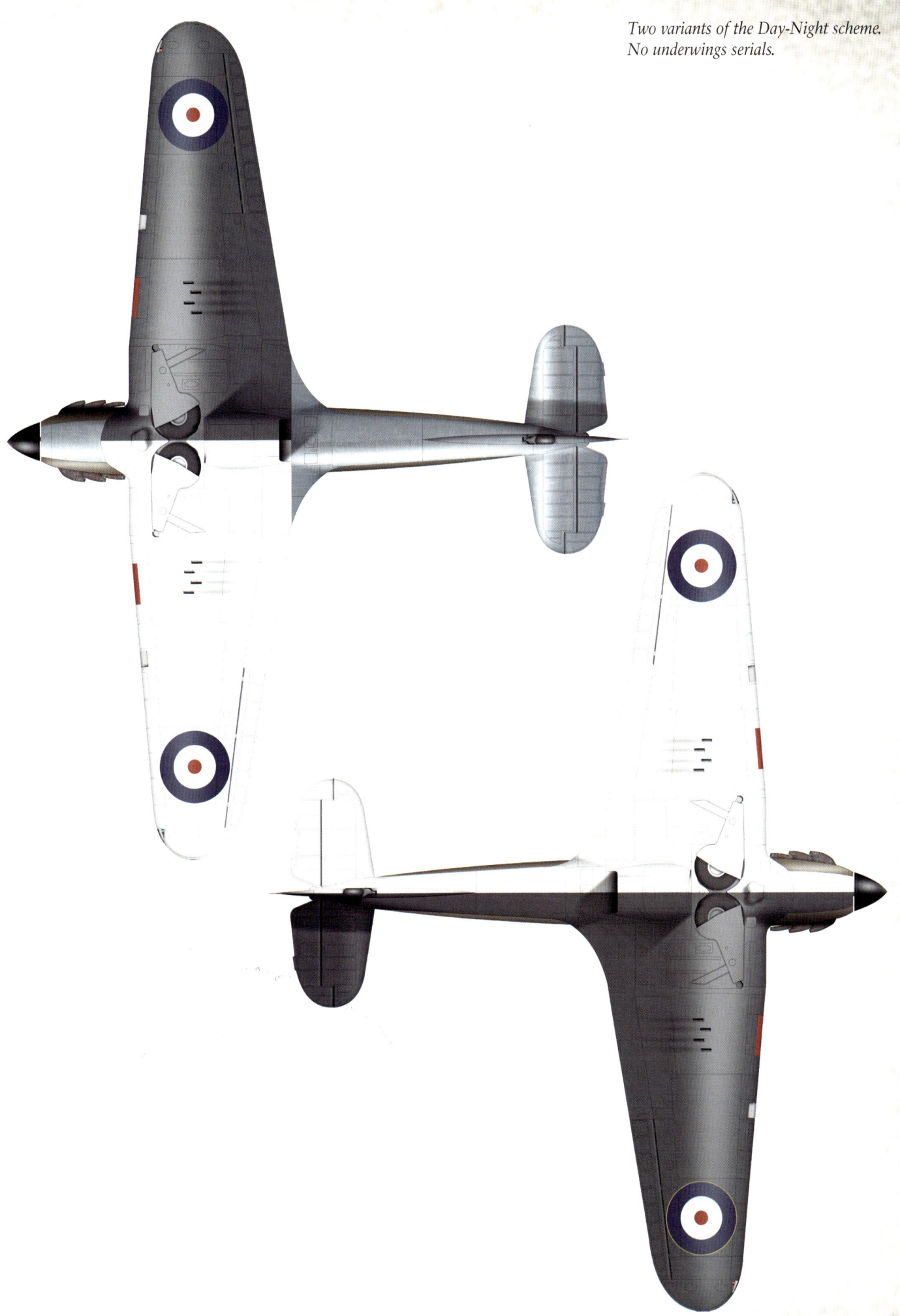

Two variants of the Day-Night scheme. No underwings serials.

Two variants with Sky undersurfaces as was used during BoB and till August 1941.

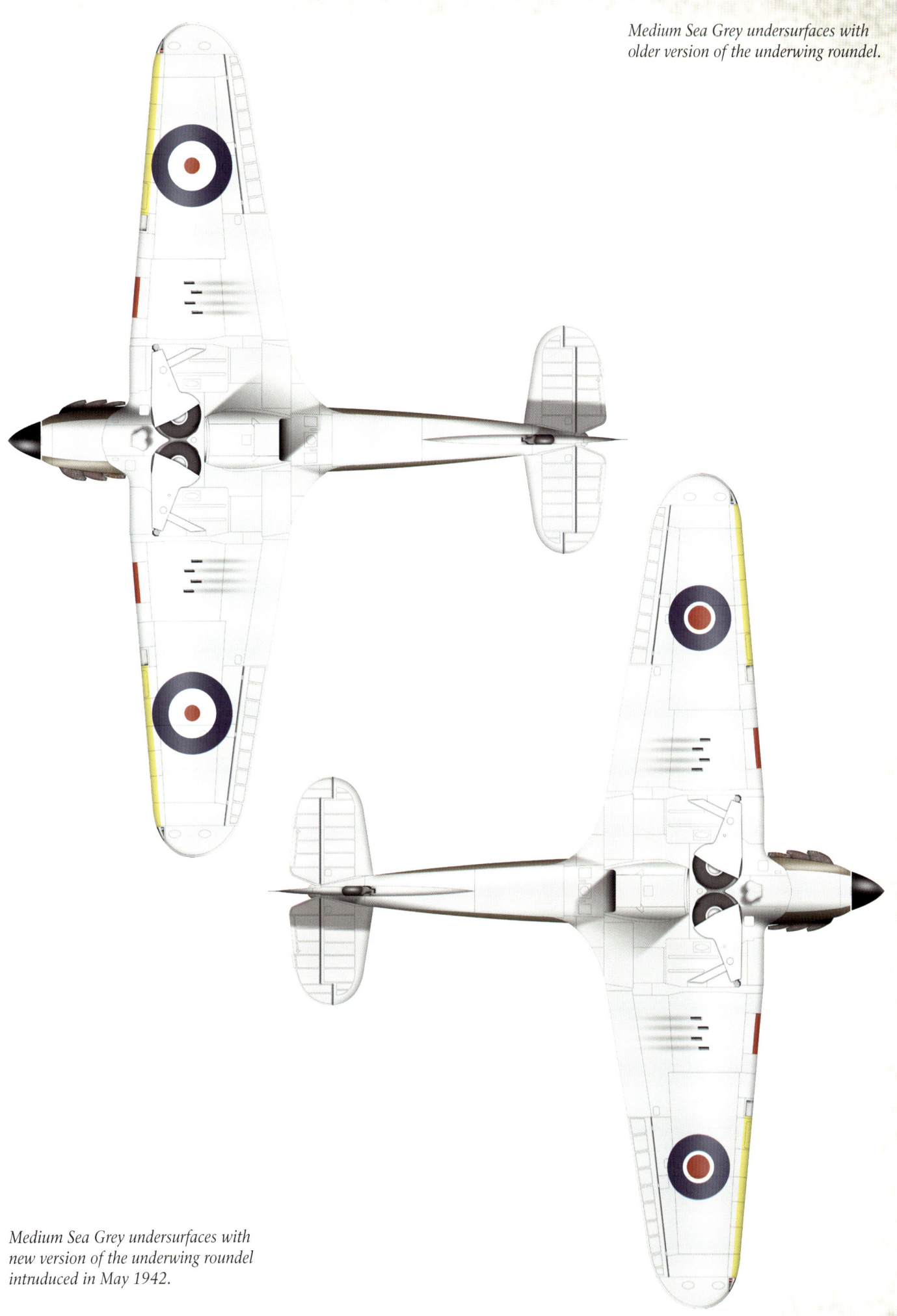

Medium Sea Grey undersurfaces with older version of the underwing roundel.

Medium Sea Grey undersurfaces with new version of the underwing roundel intruduced in May 1942.

27

Hurricane Mk I, serial L1716, AL•D of 79 Sqn RAF at Biggin Hill, August 1939. Aircraft was usually flown by F/O J. W. E. Davies. Standard RAF camouflage of the period. Dark Green and Dark Earth uppersurfaces with Day/Night undersurfaces. Fuselage roundel only in Red and Blue.

Hurricane Mk I, serial N2358, Z of 1 Sqn RAF at Vassincourt, France in October 1939. F/O "Pussy" Palmer flew this aircraft. Later this Hurricane was exported to Finland and was marked as HC-457. Crashed on June 3rd 1940 by V. Pinomaa at Turk airfield. Dark Green and Dark Earth uppersurfaces with Day/Night undersurfaces.

Hurricane Mk I, serial P2569, D of 73 Sqn RAF. Aircraft was normally flown by F/Lt R. E. Lovett. Rouvress, France, April 1940. Dark Green and Dark Earth uppersurfaces with Day/Night undersurfaces.

Hurricane Mk I, serial V1718, UZ•V of 306 Sqn RAF (Polish). Ternhill, UK, March 1941. Dark Green and Dark Earth uppersurfaces with Day/Night undersurfaces. [Further Polish Hurricane information in: "Polish Fighter Colours 1939-1947: Volume 1" ISBN: 978-83-63678-62-3.]

29

Hurricane Mk IA, serial V6697, DT•A of 257 Sqn RAF. Personal aircraft of Robert R. Stanford-Tuck, squadron commander. North Weald, December 1940. Dark Green and Dark Earth uppersurfaces with Sky undersurfaces, port wing underside black. Note that serial number was repeated under the horizontal tailplane in 3 inch letters.

Hurricane Mk IA, serial P31210, RF•A of 302 Sqn RAF (Polish). Northolt, September 1940. Dark Green and Dark Earth uppersurfaces with Sky undersurfaces.. Note diagonal band on the rear fuselage probably red, as depicted, or black.

Hurricane Mk IA, serial P3143, Gloster built machine, NN•D of 311 (Czech) Sqn. On 16 October 1940 this aircraft crashed and pilot F/Sgt J. Chalupa was killed. Dark Green and Dark Earth uppersurfaces Sky undersurfaces.

31

Hurricane Mk I (Trop), serial P2544, YK•T of 71 OTU RAF (a former aircarft of 274 Sqn). On June 6th, 1941 was severely damaged after a forced landing at Ismailia. Dark Green and Dark Earth uppersurfaces Azure Blue undersurfaces.

Hurricane Mk I (Trop), serial P3731, J of 261 SQN RAF. usualy flown by Sgt F.N. Robertson, Malta, December 1940. Dark Earth and Mid Stone uppersurfaces Azure Blue undersurfaces.

Standard Azure Blue undersurfaces.

Hurricane Mk I (Trop), serial Z4230, 4 of of GC Alsace, flown by P/O Mailfert Maaten-Baguish June 1942, North Africa. Dark Earth and Mid Stone uppersurfaces Azure Blue undersufaces. Free French markings.

Hurricane Mk X Trop, serial AG224 of SAAF Central Flying School at Norton, South Rhodesia. 1946. Aluminium dope overall with black anti-glare panel.

Hurricane Mk I, serial P2992 P of 247 Sqn RAF. Hornchurch 1943. High-visibility Red overall.

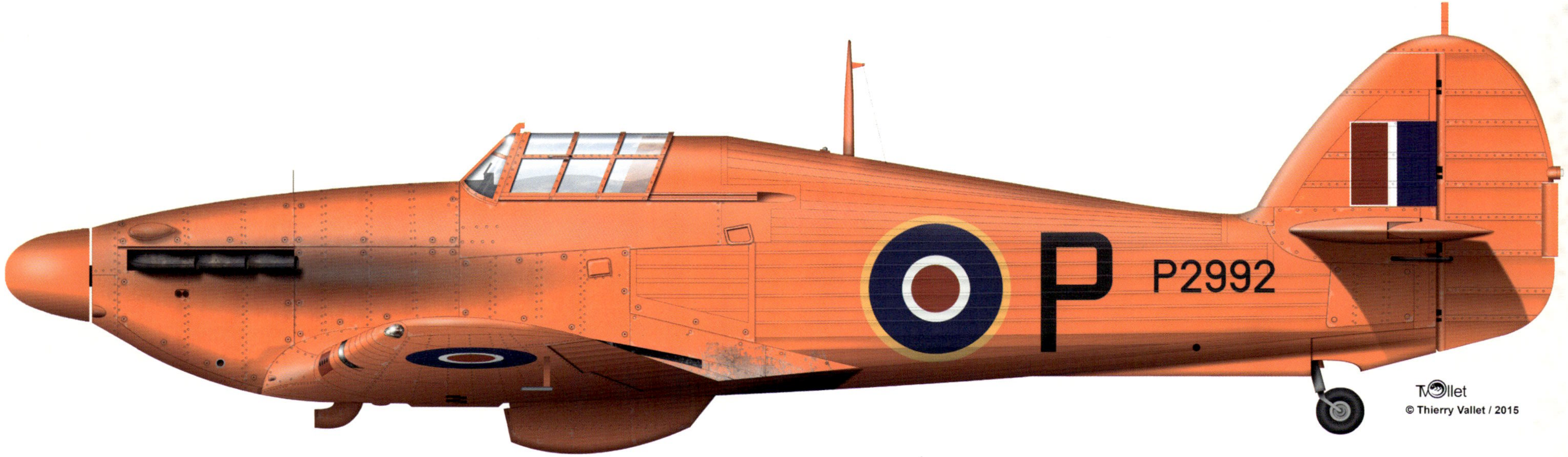

Hurricane Mk I, serial L2006 Y of 6 OTU, 11 Group Pilot Pool, RAF Sutton Bridge, August 1942. Dark Green and Dark Earth uppersurfaces Yellow undersurfaces. Red fuselage band.

Hurricane Mk I, HC-454, 2/Lentolaivue 26, Finnish Air Force, Kilpasilta airfield, April 1943. Olive Green and Black uppersurfaces Light Blue-grey undersurfaces, serial and spinner Black. [Further Finnish Hurricane information in: "Finnish Fighter Colours 1939-1945: Volume 2" ISBN: 978-8363678449.]

35

Hurricane Mk Ia, serial P2683 (?), DF+SC, captured by the Germans in France after a forced landing by P/O R. M. S. Roddy-Rayner of 87 Sqn RAF on May 19th 1940, Lille. Aircraft was used at Rechlin and later in different German Aviation schools before crashing in August 1943. Dark Green and Ocean Grey uppersurfaces with fuselage sides in RLM 02 with blotches of RLM 70 and RLM 04 undersurfaces.

Hurricane Mk I, No. 15, of Eskadrila 53, Grupul 5 Vanatore, Saltz airfield, July 1941. No. 15 was one of the three Yugoslav (Zmaj-built) Hurricanes captured by the Germans in 1941 and sold to Romania. The plane was lost on 6 September 1941 during a ground attack by Soviet fighters on Saltz airfield. Ex-Yugoslav Hurricanes Nos. 13, 14 and 15 in service with Escadrila 53 featured visible differences from the Romanian Hurricanes: windshield without horizontal frame, or rearview mirror and fitted with fabric-covered wings. Armament was eight 7.9 mm Belgian-made FN Browning machine guns. The Zmaj-built Hurricanes were camouflaged with Dark Green (FS 34096), Light Earth (FS 30118) and Dark Brown (FS 20040) on upper-surfaces and with light grey-blue under-surfaces (FS 25526). (See page 63)

Mk IIA Series 1

One of the lessons of the Battle of Britain was the low effectiveness of machine guns in comparison with cannon. Although this risk had been foreseen before the war, a suitable cannon was not found in time. It became clear that re-equipment of Hurricanes with 20 mm cannon would became necessary. As a result, it was highly desirable to install a more powerful engine, as the existing Merlin did not provide a sufficient power excess to keep the aircraft's performance with the greater weight of the proposed armament. The solution appeared to be the Merlin XX engine fitted with a two-speed supercharger and rated at 1,319 hp (989 kW) at sea level and 3,000 rpm, 1,460 hp (1,095 kW) at 6,250 ft (1,905 m) at the same rpm number and 1,435 hp (1,076 kW) at 3,000 rpm and at 11,000 ft (3,353 m). The engine was fitted with a Rotol RS 5/2 airscrew of 11 ft 3 in (3.429 m) diameter.

The first Merlin XX, serial C9873, arrived at Langley in April 1940 and was promptly installed in the Hurricane Mk I P3269. On June 11 the aircraft was test flown by Lucas. Because the new engine was slightly longer than the previous one, it was necessary to modify the engine mount and cowlings. Trials of the prototype were carried out at Boscombe Down; the machine achieved a maximum speed 348 mph at 17,402 ft (560 kph at 5,304 m) . For the moment the armament was unchanged. The next 13 machines were built to the same configuration. The Air Ministry decided not to wait for the planned armament increase and immediately ordered production aircraft, which – designated Hurricane Mk IA Series I – appeared in combat units in September 1940. The first unit equipped with the new aircraft was 111 Sqn, the same unit that had inaugurated the Hurricane Mk I into service with the RAF. However, the new aircraft did not see any action in the Battle of Britain.

The Hurricanes IIA Series I showed little difference to the Mk I except a slightly lengthened fuselage just in front of pilot's cockpit and new exhaust pipes (although these did not appear on all aircraft). In the first production batches the new machines were built using existing airframes originally intended for the earlier version. This was because the Air Ministry wanted to have the new version of the fighter in service as quickly as possible. Just after the tests on P3269 the another ten Mk Is were rebuilt in the same way and then 40 more. (Approximately – it seems no-one can give the exact number of aircraft rebuilt to the Mk II version. Some sources give the number as 100 aircraft.) Part of this batch was sent to Russia, instead of the originally intended Spitfires.

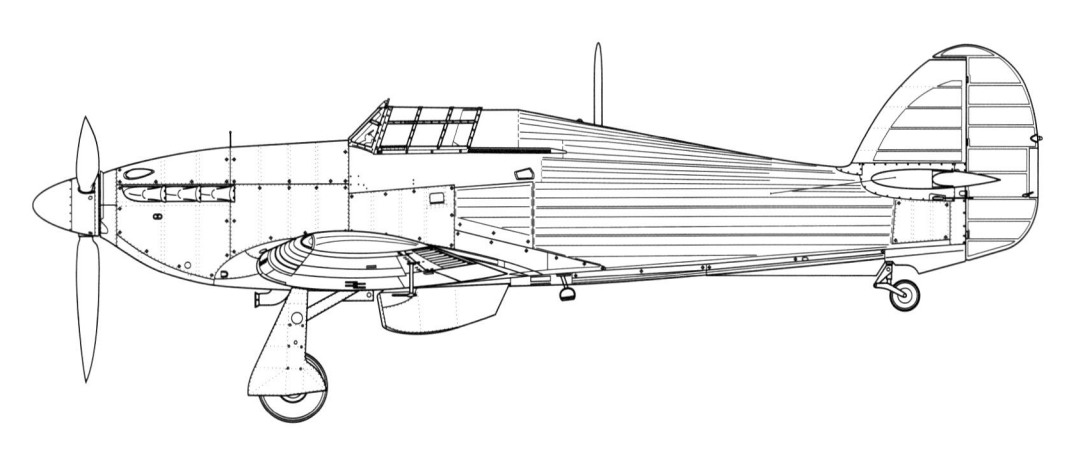

Mk IIA Series 2

Together with the introduction of the Mk II version it was decided to implement Camm's idea, from January 1940, of installing four additional Browning machine guns in modified wings, to increase the total number of guns to twelve. The aircraft was designated Hurricane Mk IIA Series 2, and was put into production at the end of 1940. The first machines came from the batch ordered from the Austin Motor Company plant in Longbridge (however, some sources state that these aircraft were of IIB and IIC versions). The plant had already opened a new production line, where it was planned to build 300 Hurricanes with Merlin XX engine. Almost two-thirds of the aircraft built there were sent to the USSR, and the rest to the Middle East.

The characteristic feature of Longbridge-built aircraft was that they were tropicalised and fitted with Vokes air filters. Other than the standard tropical equipment (as described for the Mk I version) the coolant tank was enlarged. This caused an additional lengthening of the front fuselage part by approximately 6.5 in (16.5 cm). The longer fuselage, with the Vokes filter installed, caused a shift of the centre of gravity forward, and as a result some instability and tendency to nose-over on the ground. As a result, the installation of an enlarged tank was abandoned, and the lengthened fuselage was left as a small batch of twelve Mk IIA Series 2 aircraft. (This is contrary to a substantial number of sources that state the aircraft that had slightly lengthened fuselages were Mk IIA Series 1 and not Series 2.) Unfortunately, a shortage of machine guns meant that it was impossible to install the planned armament, and the new aircraft were armed with the standard eight guns. Aircraft of this version were built later by other plants in both "tropical" and "temperate" variants.

Besides the aforementioned modifications, the Mk IIA Series 2 aircraft were fitted with Rotol RS 5/2 airscrews, a new design tailwheel leg, and provision for additional fuel tanks under the wings.

Hurricane Mk II of 630 Sqn. (Robert Gretzyngier)

Gloster built Hurricane Mk II BG827 of 273 Sqn, Katukurunda, Ceylon, used for coastal shipping protection in 1942. (Robert Greztyngier)

Mk IIB

Twelve machine guns were installed only in the next version, which was designated Mk IIB. An additional four machine guns were mounted in pairs in each outer wing. However, the wing chord this far out was narrower, and thus the barrels of these additional Brownings protruded slightly from the leading edge. Except for the armament, the Mk IIB version was the same as the Mk IIA Series I. The increased armament introduced in the Mk IIB was not popular with pilots, despite the extra hitting power. Because of this, combat units sometimes removed one pair of Brownings, which reduced the number of guns to ten. Sometimes all four additional machine guns were removed, which made the aircraft effectively identical to the Mk IIA version.

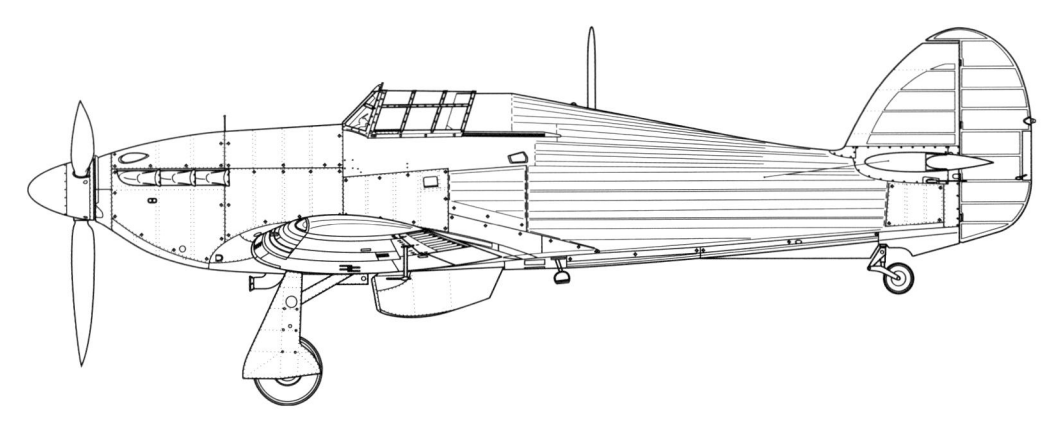

Hurricane IIBs of 151 Wing RAF, Murmansk area, Russia, November 1941. (Stratus coll.)

Mk IIB "Hurribomber"

As early as November 1940 the idea of fitting the Hurricane with underwing racks for bombs was explored in the Hawker design office, with a view to including ground attack missions in the Hurricane's tasks. Comprehensive tests of the bomb rack set-up were performed in May 1941 at the A&AEE, Boscombe Down. The aircraft used for tests carried two 250 lb (113 kg) bombs and had the wing armament reduced to ten machine guns.

As a result of the Boscombe Down tests, a batch of production Hurricanes was adapted for the installation of bomb racks and bomb release gear. Instead of the 250 lb bombs, the aircraft could carry a pair of 500 lb (227 kg) bombs or 44, 45 gal (200, 205 l) and, in the case of long-range ferry flights, 90 gal (409 l) underwing fuel tanks. Only the 44 gal (200 l) tanks could be jettisoned in flight; the other two types were fixed. With the bombs, the aircraft were quickly nicknamed "Hurribombers". The wing armament of these machines was also reduced to ten or eight machine guns.

39

Hurricane Mk IIB
1/72 scale.

Hurricane Mk IIB, "Hurribomber" 1/72 scale.

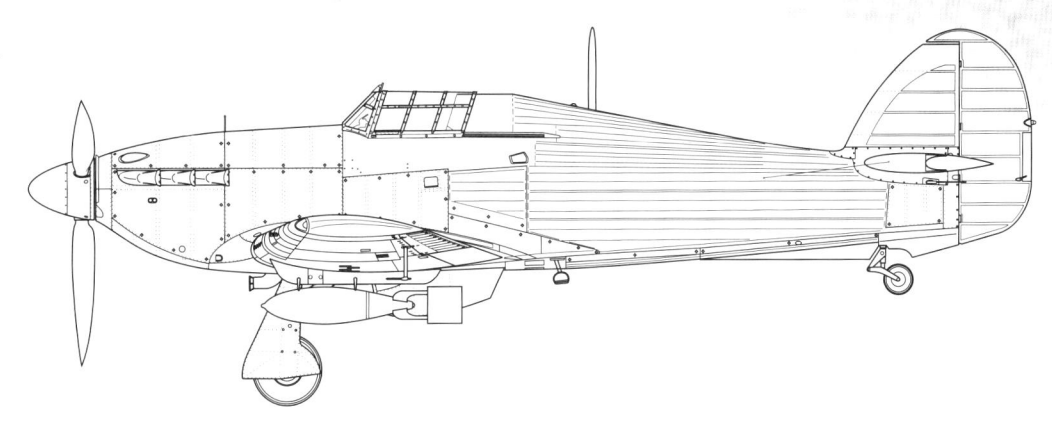

Mk IIC

The desired armament upgrade of four Hispano 20mm cannon appeared first in the Mk IIC Hurricane. The prototype of this version was a standard Mk I, P2640, fitted with wings enabling the installation of four 20 mm British Hispano Mk I cannon, but was initially built without the guns installed. The increase of airframe weight, without any parallel engine power increase, meant that the performance dropped significantly. The aircraft was tested by 151 Sqn at North Weald.

Soon new wings with cannon were installed in Mk Is V7260, V7360 and W9324. All three were transferred to Boscombe Down for tests, and an official report described them as Hurricanes IIC, although it is very doubtful that they were also fitted with Merlin XX engines. Due to inadequate performance they were not treated as potential combat machines but only as test beds, for example V7360 was

Bombs being fitted to the racks. Also of note is the box-like camera gun mounting on the wing leading edge. (IWM)

Hawker Langley built Mk IIC intruder Hurricane BE500 of 87 Sqn's Commanding Officer Sqn Ldr D.G. Smallwood, when based at Charmy Down and St Mary's in 1942. (Robert Gretzyngier)

later used for tests of cannon compartment cooling.

The first proper Hurricane Mk IIC aircraft were V2461, Z2588, Z2885 and Z2891 fitted with the Merlin XX engines and the new wings. However, for comparison tests both Hispano cannon and Oerlikon cannon were trialled, each in different machines. Aircraft with the latter armament later went into production, although the number of Oerlikon-armed Hurricanes was much smaller than Hispano-equipped ones, and many of those were re-armed with Hispano cannon during overhauls. As well as the increased firepower, the machine was fitted with the same modifications for provision for underwing fuel tanks or bombs as the Mk IIB.

The combination of new cannon armament and the more powerful engine gave excellent results. During the flight tests of the prototypes at the A&AEE the maximum speed of the Hurricane Mk IIC was 335 mph at 16,600 ft (540 kph at 5,060 m) and take-off weight 7,880 lb (3,574 kg). During tests, the two machines were fitted with Vokes tropical filters and their performance was measured once again, resulting in 320 mph at 16,200 ft (515 kph at 4,938 m). The drop in speed was thus quite small.

Delivery of Mk IIC aircraft started in April 1941, the first squadrons to receive the new fighters being 3 Sqn at Martlesham Heath and 257 Sqn at Coltishall. At the end of production in September 1944, the total of all factory production was approximately 4,711 Mk IIC aircraft. It remains unknown, however, how many aircraft of other marks were rebuilt to Mk IIC standard, and if there were also Canadian licence-built Mk XII Hurricanes among them. This was the most widespread Hurricane version used throughout the war – by 80 RAF squadrons.

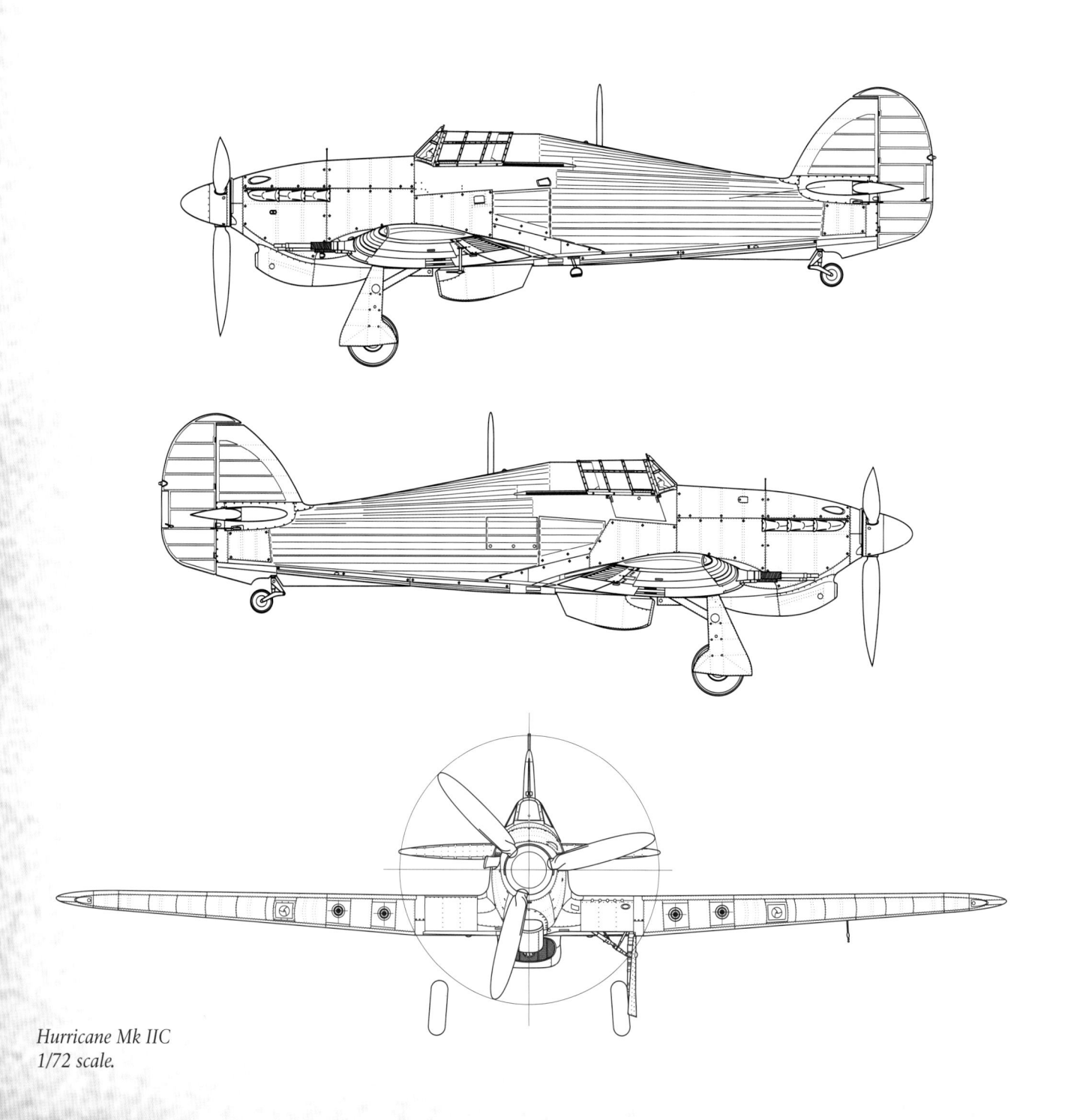

Hurricane Mk IIC
1/72 scale.

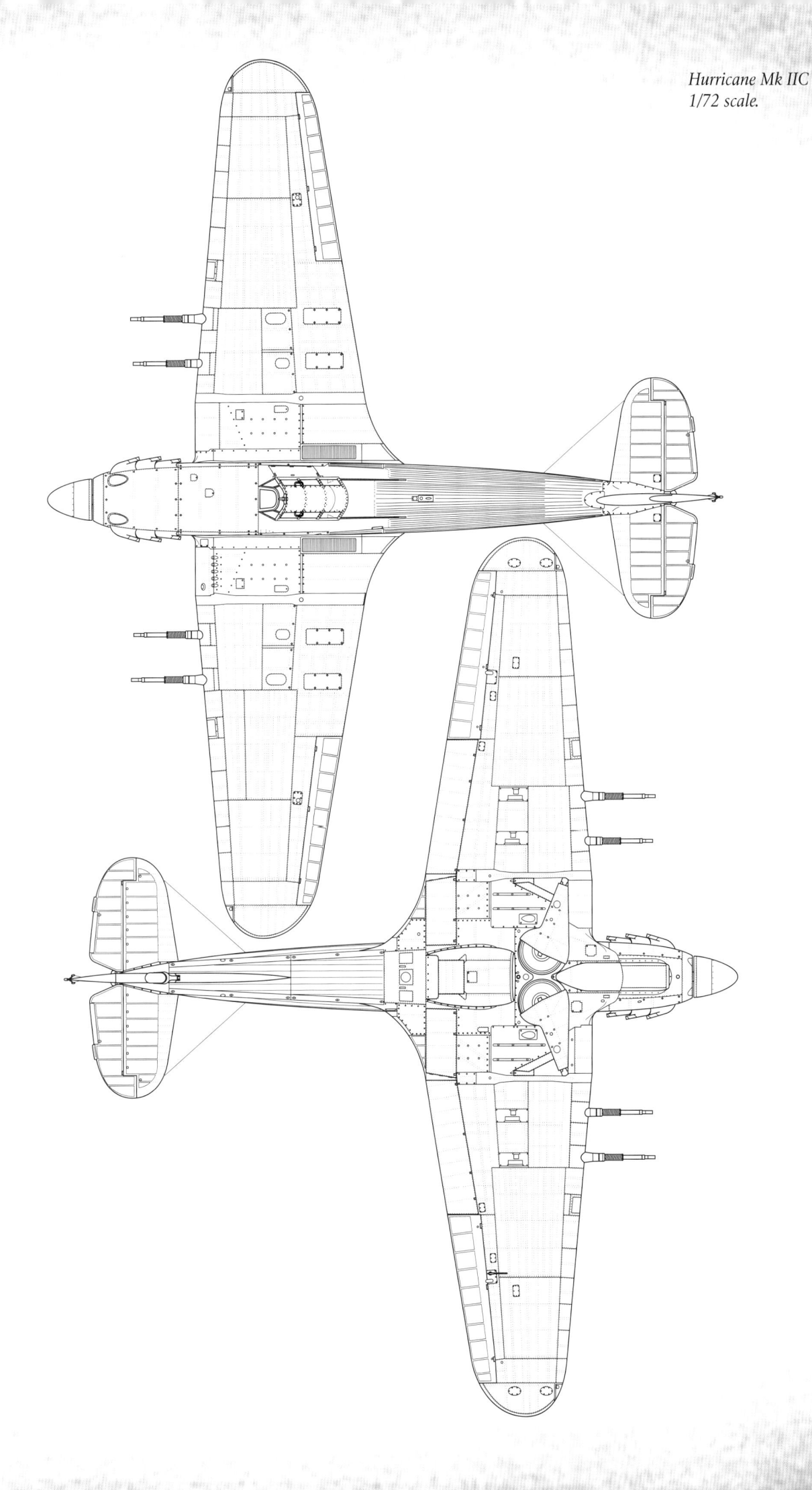

*Hurricane Mk IIC
1/72 scale.*

MK IID

At about the time the Hurricanes was being replaced in front-line fighter units by Spitfires, it became clear that Hurricanes would be useful in specialised ground attack missions. The Hurricane had been used on an ad-hoc ground attack basis before (and with good results), however, the 20 mm Hispano cannon were ineffective against tank armour. Nevertheless, the aircraft's structure – the archaic framework covered with fabric – had an advantage: it was very hard to cause structural damage. With this fact in consideration, it was decided to build a special anti-tank version. First the armament was increased with two designs of cannon developed in parallel, one by Vickers and one by Rolls-Royce. Both types were 40 mm calibre. The Vickers "S" type cannon was intensively tested on a Vickers Armstrong Wellington.

Two Vickers "S" guns, with 15 rounds per gun, were installed in aerodynamic pods under the wings of Hurricane Mk IIA Series 2 Z2326, which also had the standard armament removed except for two machine guns (which were armed with tracers and used for sighting purposes). In this form the aircraft was test-flown by K. G. Seth-Smith on September 18th, 1941, at Boscombe Down. It became the prototype of the Mk IID Hurricane. After a series of tests the aircraft went to Farnborough and later returned to Langley, where the "S" cannon were replaced with BF 40s made by Rolls-Royce. It turned out that the Rolls-Royce gun was less reliable than the Vickers, prone to jam and in addition had a smaller magazine with only 12 rounds per gun. The trials finished when one of the RR cannon failed. The Vickers cannon was then therefore selected for production machines.

The first Mk IIDs arrived at front-line units at the beginning of March 1942. Other than the armament, they did not differ from the fighter mark, having identical armour and fittings. After 92 aircraft were built, it was decided to install better protection for the pilot by adding 368 lb (167 kg) of armour.

Almost all Mk IIDs were tropicalised as standard, and equipped with Vokes filters. Of approximately 300 built, most were sent to the Middle East and Africa, where they were intensively used. The first machines arrived in April 1942 and were allocated to 6 Sqn in Shandur, Egypt. However, as only a few new machines were available, the first aircraft were only used for training. The aircraft left in the UK (mostly fitted with less armour) were delivered to 164 and 186 Sqns.

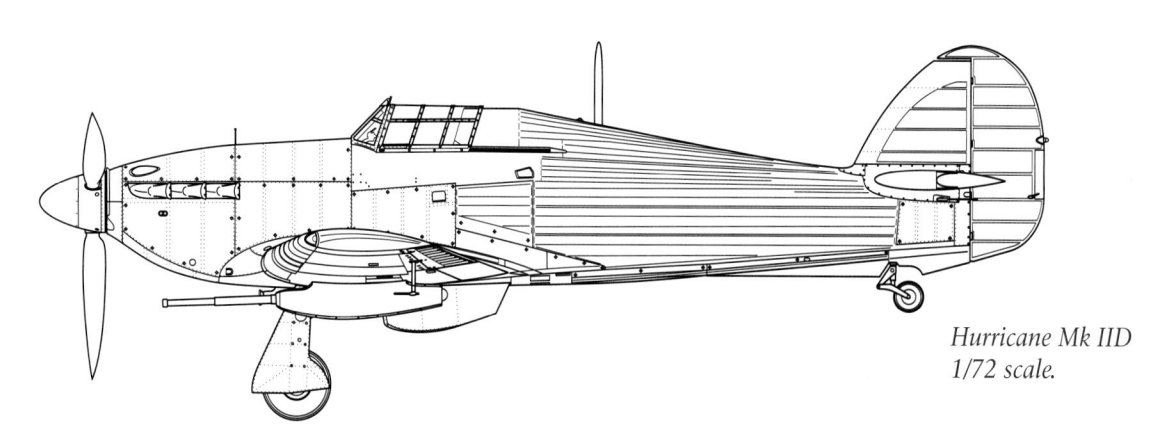

Hurricane Mk IID 1/72 scale.

Official and unofficial Mk II Variations

Mk II Trop

This version was similar to the Mk I Trop, and intended for operations outside Europe in the Middle East, Africa, and Asia. Mostly modified on the production line, and not in the field.

NF Mk IIC

In comparison with the NF Mk I, the NF IIC was better prepared for night missions only in respect of its more effective armament. Obviously, this increased gunnery effectiveness, but luck, rather than skill and tactics, directed the results. Part of the problem was the large size and weight of the early airborne interception radars (AI) which were too bulky for installation in single-seat single-engine fighters.

One interesting idea for using such fighters without their own radar was the Turbinlite teams proposed by Wing Commander W. Helmore at the end of 1940. A Douglas Havoc was fitted with a powerful spotlight in the nose, and carried radar. The Havoc was accompanied by two Hurricanes, which aimed to stay close to the Havoc to undertake the attack. To facilitate this challenging formation flying, white stripes were applied to the Havoc's wings.

When an enemy formation was detected by ground radar stations, the Havoc's pilot was directed towards them. When the formation leader in the Havoc obtained the radar echo of an intruder, he closed in and at a distance of about 300 yards switched on the spotlight, illuminating the target. Then the escorting Hurricanes could attack the spot-lit bomber.

Everything was very neat in theory. However, in practice, the Turbinlite idea failed. A night flight in close formation, often in complete darkness, required almost superhuman flying and visual abilities. Unfortunately, not all pilots were even trained to an adequate standard for night flying, and several fighter and Havoc teams were lost. This might have been acceptable if the losses had been compensated for with successes. However that was not the case – the first "victory" was an RAF Short Stirling bomber returning from a raid over Germany.

Usually, the Hurricanes taking-off for a rendezvous with the Havoc could not even find it. When a formation managed to form up, if the Havoc was lucky enough to find and light up the enemy, the Hurricane pilots were also dazzled and an intruder could escape.

Ten fighter squadrons took part in Turbinlite operations. However, when the first attempts failed, the entire experiment was abandoned in 1943, as by then radar-equipped Beaufighters and Mosquitos were available.

Hurricane Mk IIC BE500 breaks away from the camera aircraft to show the underside. Originally marked with underwing roundels, these have been painted over. (Robert Gretzyngier)

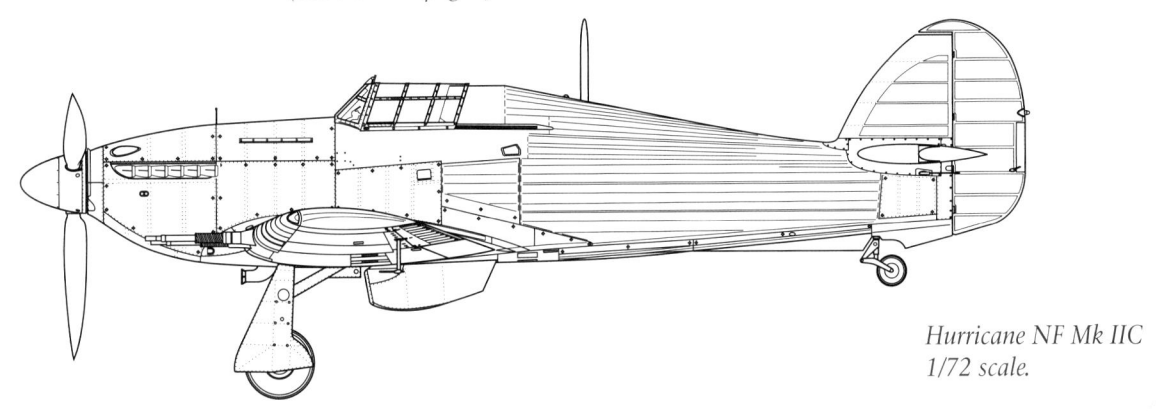

Hurricane NF Mk IIC 1/72 scale.

"Met. Mk II"

The Hurricane Met. Mk II was in fact a Mk IIC with meteorological equipment installed instead of guns. The aircraft flew usually up to heights of 24,600 ft (7,500 m) collecting details at each 1,000 ft height. Data collected during such missions was used for the preparation of weather reports.

"Tac R. Mk II"

The first Mk II (A & B) Hurricanes landed in North Africa in 1941. During the repair of damaged machines in field workshops, some of them were modified as tactical reconnaissance machines in the same way as the Mk I had been. The first recorded use of a Tac R. Mk II aircraft took place in February 1942, with 6 Sqn at Helwan. Soon reconnaissance Hurricanes were delivered to 451 RAAF, 208 RAF and 7 and 40 Sqns South African Air Force (SAAF). Some aircraft flew without armament, but others retained their guns. Tac R. Mk II Hurricanes were fitted with two vertical F.24 8in cameras installed just behind the pilot's cockpit.

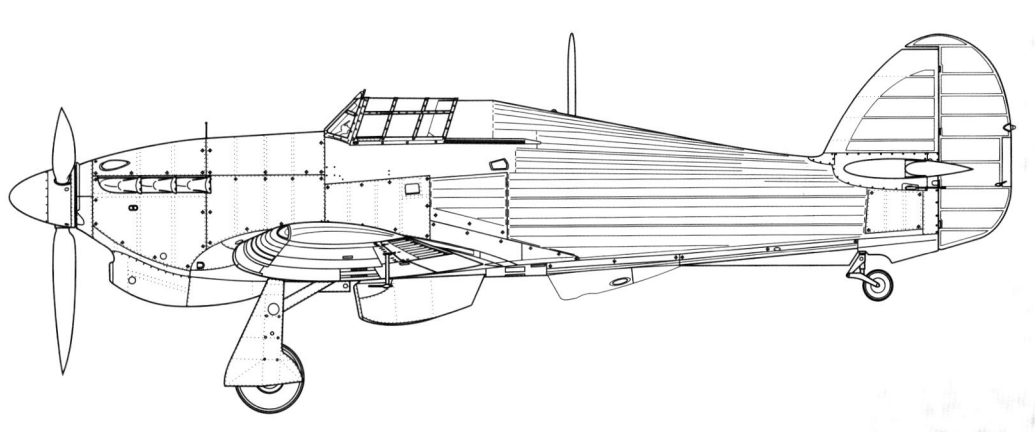

"PR Mk II"

Hurricane PR Mk IIs were similar to PR Mk Is. Thanks to the improved Merlin engine they could fly at 34,120 ft (10,400m), with a maximum speed of 350 mph (563 kph). Their range, with additional wing tanks, was 1,100 miles (1,770 km) or five hours at economical cruise. Maximum ceiling was about 38,000 ft (11,580 m). Eighteen PR Mk II Hurricanes were built.

Mk III

A version of the Hurricane, largely similar to the Mk II but with a Packard-built Merlin 28 engine, was planned and designated Mk III. This was a contingency against a shortage of Rolls-Royce built Merlins, which in the end never transpired. As a result the Mk III was not required.

Mk IV

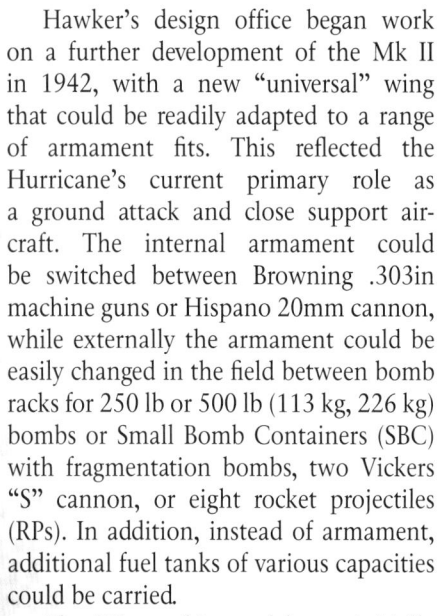

Hawker's design office began work on a further development of the Mk II in 1942, with a new "universal" wing that could be readily adapted to a range of armament fits. This reflected the Hurricane's current primary role as a ground attack and close support aircraft. The internal armament could be switched between Browning .303in machine guns or Hispano 20mm cannon, while externally the armament could be easily changed in the field between bomb racks for 250 lb or 500 lb (113 kg, 226 kg) bombs or Small Bomb Containers (SBC) with fragmentation bombs, two Vickers "S" cannon, or eight rocket projectiles (RPs). In addition, instead of armament, additional fuel tanks of various capacities could be carried.

The IIE, as this model was initially designated, was a dedicated ground attack machine, the first Hurricane intended as such from the outset. As a result it had increased armour protection for the pilot and the internal mechanics, particularly the radiator. The extra weight and drag necessitated an increase in power and a Merlin 27 of 1,620 hp was chosen as a suitable powerplant. As the aircraft differed considerably in some areas from the Mk II, a new designation of Mk IV was applied.

Testing on the Mk IV's armament fit had begun with rocket projectile trials with modified Mk IIA Z2415, later replaced with Mk IV BP173, at Boscombe Down in August 1942, with generally good results. The RPs were devastatingly effective against many ground targets, but they caused the handling and stability of the Hurricane to deteriorate somewhat at low speeds. For take-off and high speed flight, handling was remarkably little affected, especially considering the Hurricane Mk IV was, fully loaded, some 2,000lb heavier than an early Mk I.

Hurricane Mk IV 6 Sqn, Greece 1944/45. (IWM CNA 3198)

Confusingly, the first true Mk IV was finished with a Merlin 32 and four blade propeller – features that would later reappear on the stillborn Mk V. However, the propeller was soon changed to a Rotol RS 5/11 3-blade unit, as the four blade item exacerbated instability at lower speeds.

The Hurricane Mk IV was considered to be ideal for operations in theatres such as the Middle East, North Africa and Asia, so many were factory-fitted with Vokes filters and tropical equipment. It was delivered to seven squadrons in the UK, two squadrons in the Mediterranean area, and two in Burma, which made a major contribution to speeding the end of the war in Asia by harrying Japanese forces and preventing counter attacks. After withdrawal from front-line units the aircraft were used for secondary tasks, such as radar calibration or training. However, although it was successful in combat the Mk IV was not such a "pilot's aircraft" as earlier versions, as the increase in weight had blunted the fine handling and performance somewhat. The Mk IV

*Hurricane Mk IV
1/72 scale.*

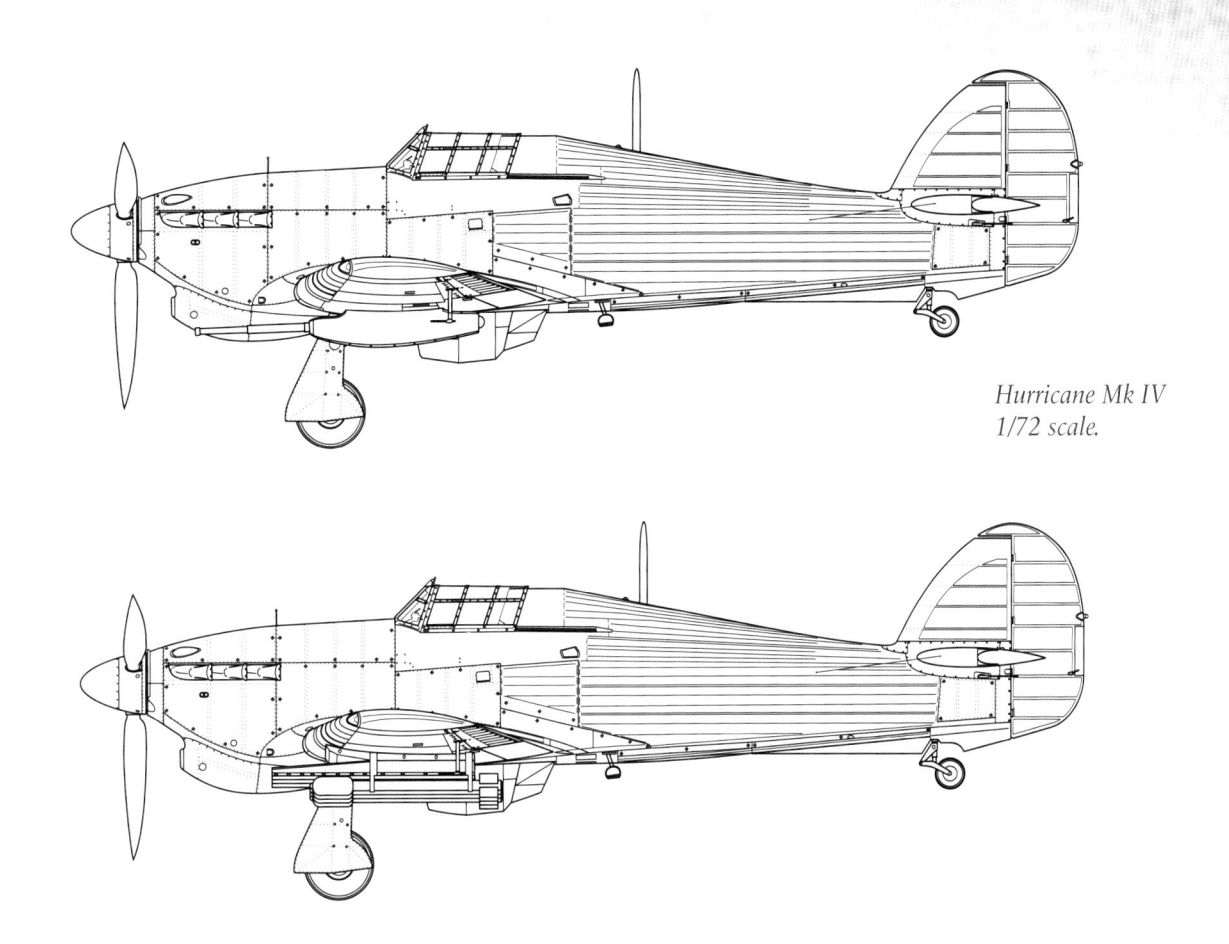

Hurricane Mk IV of the Balkan Air Force, 1944. Note the asymmetric underwing load. (IWM CNA 3199)

47

used no fewer than three different types of Merlin depending on availability, the 24, 27 and 32, all with a maximum output of around 1,600hp. The last proposed development of the Hurricane, a full ten years after Sydney Camm's initial "Fury Monoplane" proposals, was the Mk V. (see page 68).

A Hurricane Mk IV of 6 Squadron RAF at Foggia, 1944. (Stratus coll.)

Hurricane Mk IV, serial KX413 of 164 Squadron RAF at Middle Wallop 1943. The aircraft are equipped with 40mm Vickers S anti-tank guns. (Stratus coll.)

Hurricane Mk IV Trop serial KX802, AW•B of 42 Squadron RAF, Ondaw, Burma 1942. (IWM CF 262)

48

Hurricane Mk II Trop, serial 2827 M, Night Fighting Unit Ta' Qali, Malta 1941. Dark Earth and Mid Stone uppersurfaces Black undersurfaces.

Hurricane Mk IIB Trop, serial BG727 of Night Fighter Unit, Malta, September 1941. Night overall.

49

Hurricane Mk IIC, serial BP703, FT•O, "MAHENGE" of 43 Sqn RAF. Aircraft was generally flown by P/O Antony Snell, Tangmere, August 1942. Night overall.

Hurricane Mk IIC, serial HV538 B of 3 Sqn, RIAF, Burma 1945. Dark Green, Ocean Grey uppersurfaces Medium Sea Grey undersurfaces.

Hurricane Mk IIC, serial BN230, FT•A, of 43 Sqn RAF, Acklington, May 1942. Aircraft was generally flown by the squadron's commander Daniel Le Roy du Vivier (from Belgium). Dark Green, Ocean Grey uppersurfaces with Medium Sea Grey undersurfaces.

Hurricane Mk IIC Trop, serial HL672, AX•X of 1 Sqn SAAF, Amiriya, North Africa, end of 1942. Aircraft was mostly piloted by Capt. J. H. Gainor. Standard British Desert camouflage of Dark Earth and Middle Stone uppersurfaces and Azure Blue undersurfaces.

51

Hurricane Mk IIC Trop, serial KZ136, mO of 336 (Greek) SQN RAF. Greek pilots used Hurricanes during patrols over the Libyan coast from February 1943 until February 1944. Dark Earth and Middle Stone uppersurfaces and Azure Blue undersurfaces.

Hurricane Mk IIC Trop, serial KZ225, "49" of 1 (Indian) Service Flying and Training School at Ambala, Peshawar, 1946. Aluminium dope overall with camouflaged upper engine panels.

Hurricane Mk IIC, serial TH552, (ex PZ769) ZC of the Belgian Air Force. This machine finished its life as a technical school ground trainer. Aluminium dope overall.

Hurricane Mk IIC Trop, serial unknown, S of French Aviation School at Meknes, Marocco. In 1944 this aircraft was flown by Lt Camille Plubeau. Standard desert British camouflage but Middle Stone overpainted with Khaki or US Olive Drab.

53

Hurricane Mk IIB Trop, serial BM959, "60" of 609 IAP VVS USSR. Aircraft was shot down on 6 April 1942 close to Tiksjarvi, Karelia by Finnish pilots flying Brewster B-239s of 2/LeLV 24. Soviet pilot Ivan Babanin became POW. Aircraft in Dark Green, Ocean Grey uppersurfaces with Medium Sea Grey undersurfaces.

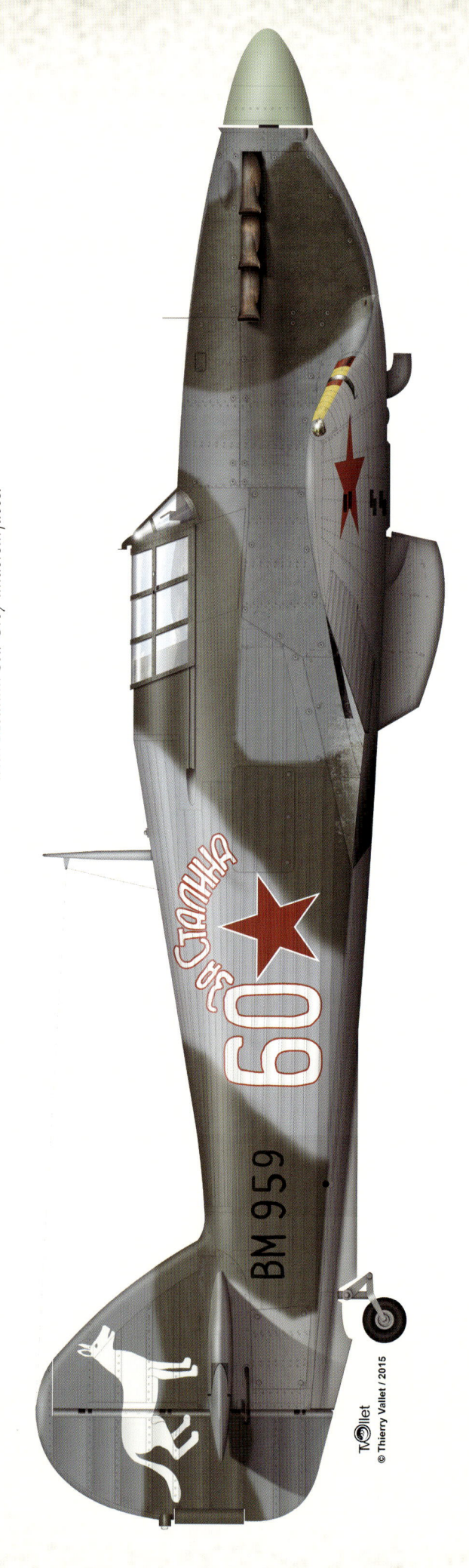

55

Hurricane Tac.R Mk IIB, serial BN125, U of 681 Sqn RAF, February 1943. PRU Blue overall.

Hurricane Mk IIB Trop, serial BE208, after capture by the Japanese. This aircraft had been the personal machine of the 232 Sqn commander, R. E. P. Brooker, at Singapore. On February 8th Brooker was shot down and force-landed. Aircraft was tested by the Tachikawa GiKen unit. Dark Green and Dark Earth uppersurfaces with Sky undersurfaces. British markings overpainted in Japanese Green colour.

Hurricane Mk IV Trop, serial KX229 H of 20 Sqn SEAC RAF, Burma 1943/44. Dark Green and Ocean Grey uppersurfaces with Medium Sea Grey undersurfaces.

Hurricane Mk IV Trop, serial KX584 BR•T of 184 Sqn RAF. Early 1944, Europe. Dark Green and Ocean Grey uppersurfaces with Medium Sea Grey undersurfaces.

Sea Hurricane

Mk IA (Catafighter)

The first carrier use by Hurricanes was when 46 Sqn's machines were loaded on board HMS Glorious on May 14th, 1940, and sailed to Norway. Due to the lack of a suitable airfield in the area held by the Allies, the aircraft carrier returned to Scotland. Glorious returned to the Norwegian coast on May 28th. Hurricanes from 46 Sqn took-off from the deck and landed at Bardufoss. After the Allied collapse, on June 8th evacuation was ordered. Rather than destroy the aircraft, the squadron's CO, Squadron Leader K B B "Bing" Cross, decided to try to land back on Glorious, despite not having arrestor hooks, and being higher-performance aircraft than any previous carrier-borne type. All eight Hurricanes landed safely, thanks to exceptional flying by the pilots, and ten Gladiators from 263 Sqn also landed aboard. Tragically, later on the same day, the ship was sunk and only 46 crew members survived, including two 46 Sqn pilots, S/L Cross and F/L "Pat" Jameson.

By this remarkable expedient it was proven that Hurricanes were able to take-off and land on aircraft carriers. Take-off was possible into a wind blowing with total speed of 43.5 mph (70 kph); landing required a wind speed of 46.6 mph (75 kph).

As a result of the desperate lack of aircraft carriers, an intermediate expedient was planned, fitting merchant ships with a catapult. This could launch a fighter for the interception of German aircraft such as the infamous Focke-Wulf Fw 200 "Condor", called "Scourge of the Atlantic" by Churchill.

The great disadvantage of this idea was its "one-shot" nature, and risks to the pilot. After launch, and hopefully a successful combat, the pilot could not land on a ship, and thus had to choose from three alternatives. If land was within range, he could try to reach it and land there. Alternatively, he could bale-out over the convoy or ditch close to the ships, and hope to be picked up. In both the latter cases the aircraft was lost.

The critical situation at sea caused this desperate plan to be put into effect. Due to the great risk the first pilots were all volunteers. Catapults were installed on HMS Maplin, Ariguani, Patia and Springbank. Each ship was equipped initially with two-seat Fairey Fulmars, and the ships were assigned to convoys in 1941. No successes were achieved, as the Fulmars were simply too slow to intercept German bombers and reconnaissance aircraft. The solution was to use Hurricanes. The first Hurricane was adapted for catapult launching in March 1941 and tested at the Royal Aircraft Establishment (RAE), Farnborough. The only difference to a standard Hurricane was the installation of catapult spools.

Successful tests resulted in fifty Mk I aircraft being transferred to repair workshops. After adaptation the machines were designated as Sea Hurricane Mk IA. The aircraft, armed with their original armament of eight .303 (7.7 mm) Browning machine guns and powered with Merlin III engines, were delivered aboard 35 selected ships. The ships were fitted with catapults installed above their fore decks. The catapult was 75 ft (24 m) long, including a 70 ft (21.3 m) long rail for the trolley carrying the aircraft. The "trolley" was propelled by solid-fuel rocket boosters, which, together with a Merlin at full throttle, gave the aircraft a speed of 75 mph (120 kph) at release. The pilot was exposed to 3.5 g acceleration.

The aircraft were technically referred to as "Catafighters" but were unofficially called "Hurricats", and the catapult-equipped ships were listed as "CAM-ships" (Catapult Armed Merchantman or Catapult Aircraft Merchantman). The first one was the Empire Rainbow, which accompanied a convoy from Halifax, Nova Scotia, to Scotland in June 1941. In the same month another five ships were put into service. Each of them carried two Hurricanes, one on the catapult and a reserve aircraft on the deck.

The training of RAF volunteer pilots was carried out at the MFSU (Merchant Ship Fighter Unit) established especially for this purpose at Speke, Liverpool, while the volunteer Fleet Air Arm (FAA) pilots trained with 804 Sqn FAA. The first victory went to Australian R W H Everett, who on August 2nd, 1941, off Sierra Leone, shot down a Fw 200. After landing close to his own ships, the pilot nearly drowned when the canopy jammed and the aircraft started to sink. As a result of this action he was gazetted with the DSO.

The amazing thing about this project is that there were so few pilot losses. Only F/L John Kendall, from HMS *Empire Morn*, was killed. He attacked a Ju 88 formation, and one of German bombers was shot down. After the combat Kendall jumped but his parachute failed to open.

Until 1943, the Hurricat pilots undertook eight missions and shot down six German aircraft. In the same period the CAM ships put to sea 175 times.

Another suggestion (which did not get beyond the concept stage) was a "piggy-backed" Hurricane aboard a Liberator, as another means of closing the Atlantic anti-Condor fighter gap

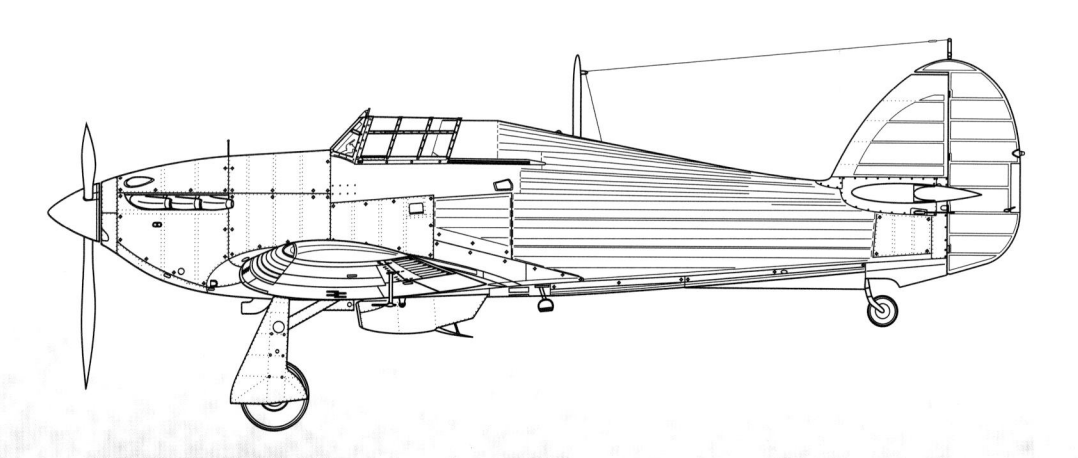

Sea Hurricane Mk IA on the catapult of Empire Tide. (IWM A 9421)

Mk IB

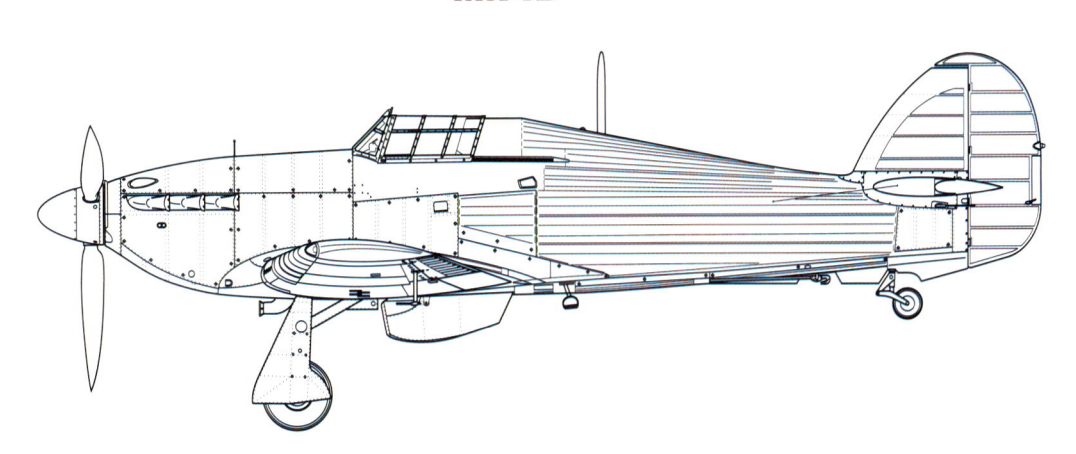

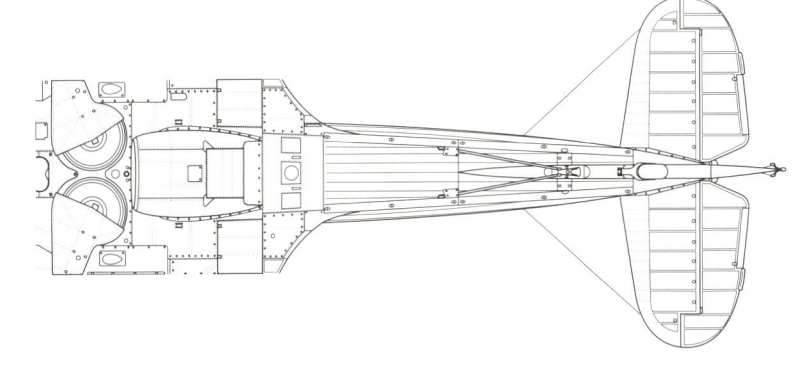

In 1943 the Royal Navy put into service MAC-ships (Merchant Aircraft Carrier). They were converted grain carriers or tankers with an added flat metal deck suitable for fighters and light bombers. This quickly provided for the large number of convoy escorts required, and thus CAM ships became superfluous.

The deck was fitted with arresting cables. Each MAC-ship had three or four aircraft on board, while the converted grain carriers had a small hangar and lift, but ex-tankers did not, and the aircraft were "spotted" (parked) permanently on the deck. The same idea was undertaken by the Americans, and in 1941 they started to convert merchant ships to MAC carriers for RN purposes. The first three were HMS *Archer*, HMS *Biter*, and HMS *Avenger*. HMS *Avenger* and its Sea Hurricanes from 802 and 883 FAA Sqns became famous during the defence of convoy PQ-18 between September 13th and 18th, 1942.

MAC-ship based Hurricanes were different to catapult-launched examples, and were designated Sea Hurricane Mk IB. They were fitted with an A-frame arrestor hook installed on the lower rear part of the fuselage frame. The CAM Hurricane catapult spools were retained, allowing launch of the aircraft from CAM-ships as well. The internal structure was strengthened. The power unit depended on which version the machine was converted from. Most IB Sea Hurricanes were rebuilt from Merlin III fitted Mk I Hurricanes, but about 26 of them were modified from Mk IIA and IIB Hurricanes with Merlin XX engines. The armament consisted always of eight machine guns.

59

Mk IC

The introduction of the Mk IIC version armed with four 20mm Hispano cannon meant that the wings of this land based version were available to fit to some Sea Hurricanes. This was finally the intended "marriage" of the Merlin III engine with 20 mm cannon, the concept earlier abandoned by the RAF. These aircraft were designated Sea Hurricane Mk IC. The first of these were delivered to FAA units in February 1942. Their performance dropped significantly, compared to the lighter armed or better engined aircraft, but for convoy escort operations this was not critical. The maximum speed amounted to 276 mph (444 kph) at 17400 ft (5,304 m).

Sea Hurricane Mk IB on HMS Victorious, *June 1942. (IWM A 10225)*

Mk IIC

Not only the wings of the Hurricane Mk IIC were given to the maritime versions. When the German forces in the Mediterranean area were increased, the damage and difficulty facing the Malta convoys increased significantly. The Admiralty asked for deliveries of rebuilt Hurricane Mk IIC aircraft with the more powerful engine and armed with four 20 mm cannon. The new version was named the Sea Hurricane Mk IIC, and had an arrestor hook but was not fitted with catapult spools.

The introduction of Mk IIC Sea Hurricanes improved the situation in the Malta battles only slightly. One of greatest combats was fought in August 1942, when more than 500 German and Italian aircraft attacked one of convoys, code name Pedestal. Seventy Sea Hurricanes of various versions took-off against the enemy and shot down 39 bombers, with the loss of eight of their own machines. Thanks to their efforts the bombs and torpedoes were mostly dropped hastily and inaccurately. However, the remaining accurate ones sank nine out of fourteen ships in the convoy.

Although Sea Hurricanes were intended for maritime service, they were also delivered to land-based squadrons. Some of these had then their arrestor hooks removed.

Mk XII

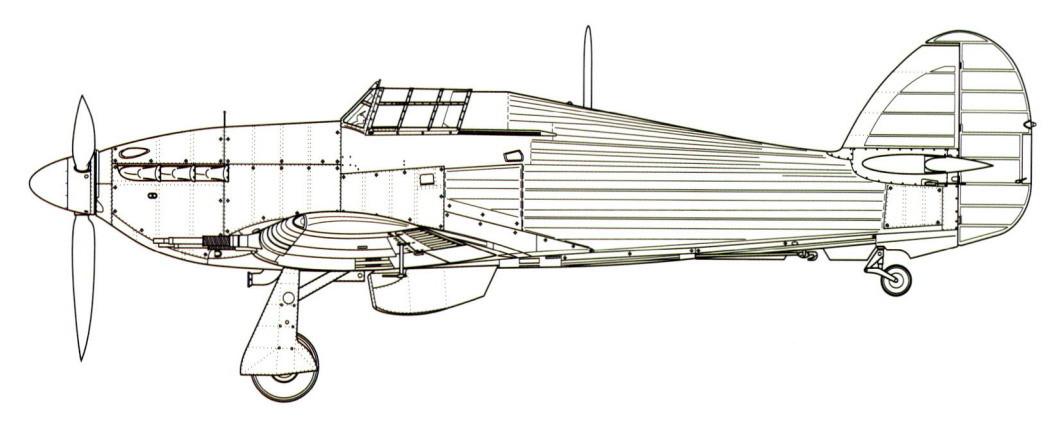

Canadian licence-built aircraft with Merlin 24 engines, and armament similar to the Sea Hurricane Mk IB. According to British sources the Sea Hurricane Mk XII was fitted with the Merlin 29 engine and armed with 12 Brownings. Unfortunately, the number of aircraft of this version delivered to the FAA is not clear.

CAM-Hurricane Mk Ia, serial V6776 NJ•L on CAM ship s/s Empire Tide's catapult, October 1941. Extra Dark Sea Grey and Dark Slate Grey uppersurfaces with Sky undersurfaces.

Sea Hurricane Mk IIB, serial AF966, 7•F of 880 Sqn FAA on HMS Indomitable in June 1942. Extra Dark Sea Grey and Dark Slate Grey uppersurfaces with Sky undersurfaces.

Licence-built versions

Belgium

Avions Fairey (Societé Anonyme Belge) Hurricane

In the late 1930s, as it became apparent that war was likely, the Belgian air force started to consider a modern replacement for its Fairey Firefly IIM and Gloster Gladiator biplanes. Despite local competition from the Renard R36, the Belgian government placed an initial order for 20 Hurricane Mk Is from Hawkers, and made arrangements for Avions Fairey to build a further 80 with armament to their own specification. Avions Fairey was well practiced at licence-building British products as the factory had been set up to construct the Firefly IIMs which had served the air force since the early 1930s. However, only a small number of aircraft had been completed by the time of the German invasion in 1940.

Licence-built Belgian Hurricane Mk Is were to have an armament of four .50in (12.65 mm) Browning FN machine guns, or two .50in Browning FN and two .303 in (7.7 mm) Brownings. The few Hurricanes built in Belgium were actually equipped with the standard British armament of eight .303 in (7.7 mm) machine guns. All but one were fitted with a two-blade Watts propeller, the exception being H-10039 which was fitted with a Rotol three-blade constant speed unit.

Yugoslavia

Ikarus "Hurrischmitt"

Yugoslavia built Hurricanes under licence at two factories, Zmaj and Rogozarski. They were essentially the same as the British examples, with different equipment such as 7.9mm (.311 in) calibre guns and metric instruments. Only twenty aircraft were built in the Zmaj factory. At the same time, engineers Ilič and Sivčev from the Ikarus factory in Zemun (near Belgrade) were working on the adaptation of the Ikarus-built IK-Z aircraft to take the Daimler Benz DB 601A engine, and it was decided to do the same with the Hurricane. Older sources state that the engine cowling was adopted from a Bf 109E; however, more recent sources say that the cowling and cooling, fuel lines and so forth were designed especially for this hybrid. Flight tests were carried out at the beginning of 1941 and it turned out that the aircraft had better take-off and flight performance than the standard Hurricane and was only slightly slower than the Bf 109E-3. (It is worth mentioning that the IK-Z was experimentally fitted with a Merlin III engine, but there was not enough time to carry out flight tests, and workers destroyed the prototype to avoid its capture by the Germans).

Ikarus "Hurrischmitt"
1/72 scale

A Yugoslav Hurricane. (Jan Vd Heuvel)

Persia

Persian trainers

In 1939, Persia (now Iran) received one aircraft, Mk I P3270 which had already served with the RAF. Delivery of further aircraft was stopped due to the outbreak of war, but soon another ten Hurricanes were dispatched to Persia with 74 Sqn RAF. In May 1940 the unit was transferred to Egypt, and its machines were left in Persia. Bizarrely, in 1946, delivery was resumed and 18 used Mk IIC Hurricanes were supplied. Sixteen of them were converted to unarmed single-seat trainers with Merlin 22 engines instead of Merlin XX. The remaining two (one of them KZ232) were rebuilt as two-seaters. Both cockpits were open and fitted only with a windscreen. Nevertheless, air turbulence behind the front cockpit made the instructor's job in the aft cockpit almost impossible, with the result that the rear cockpit was covered with a bubble hood adapted from a Tempest. All Persian Hurricanes went to the Advanced Fighter Training Group at Doshan Teppeh, east of Tehran.

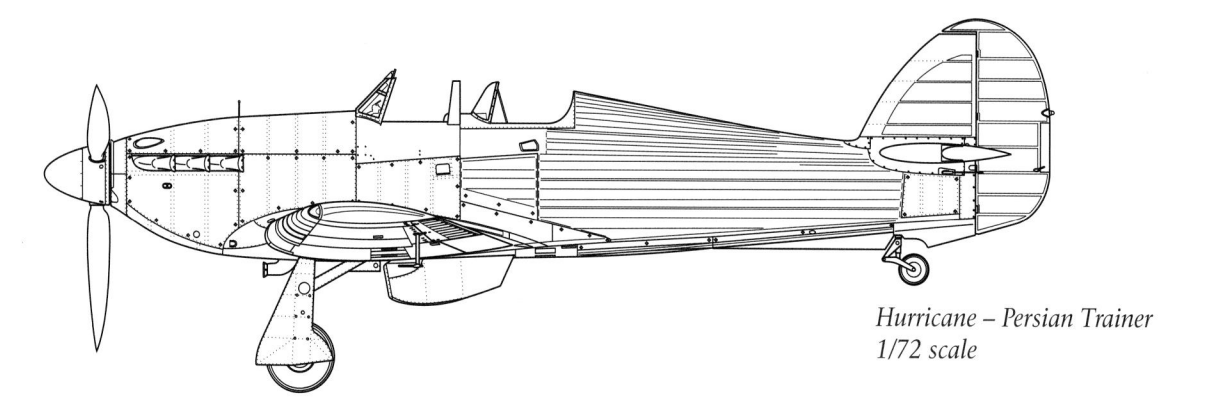

Hurricane – Persian Trainer 1/72 scale

Soviet Union

Mk IIA and IIB with Soviet armament

The firepower of IIA and IIB Hurricanes was not regarded as adequate by Soviet pilots. Instead the Brownings were removed and two (and later four) 12.7 mm (0.5 in) BS machine guns were installed. This modification was the idea of the well-know fighter pilot Boris Safonov. The experiment was successful, and Safonov decided to increase the firepower once again by the installation of two BS machine guns and two 20 mm ShVAK cannon. This armament set-up became standard for Soviet Mk IIA and IIB Hurricanes. Other known variations were four ShVAK cannon, or two with a greater ammunition capacity. Later still 12.7 mm (0.5 in) UBT machine guns were installed in combination with or without cannon.

Photo of Russian operated Hurricanes equipped with ShVAK cannon. (Stratus coll.)

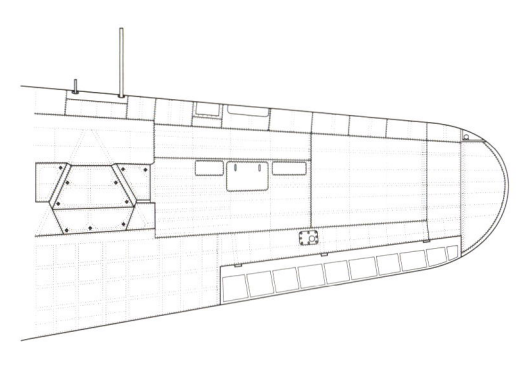

Starboard wing of the Hurricane Mk IIB with ShVAk cannon. 1/72 scale.

Russian Hurricane with ShVAK cannon during the winter. (via author)

Hurricane Mk IIA/B with RS 82 and RS 132 rockets

Safonov also proposed arming Hurricanes with four RS-82 rockets projectiles, and four (or six) rails for RS-82 (and later RS-132) rockets were installed under the wings. They were used not just against ground targets but also against aircraft. 485 IAP destroyed 13 German aircraft with rockets.

Hurricane Mk IIA/B with FAB-100 bombs

Another of Safonov's ideas was installation of two underwing racks for FAB-100 bombs. With two bombs on the racks, the aircraft's maximum speed dropped by 42 kph (26 mph).

Hurricane Mk IIC with ShVAK cannon

The installation of Soviet armament in Hurricanes was carried out at plant 81 in Moscow, although its specialists also worked in the field at nearby airfields. When Mk IIC aircraft with four Hispano cannon arrived in the USSR they usually retained their original armament, but it was sometimes replaced with four (or two) 20 mm ShVAK cannon.

Hurricane with a rear gunner

One Hurricane (Canadian-built Mk XI BW948) supplied to USSR was fitted in 1942 with an open rear gunner's position with a flexibly mounted ShKAS machine gun just behind the pilot's cockpit. The sliding canopy was removed.

Hurricane Mk IIB (UTI)

The two-seat Soviet trainer was converted by the addition of a second cockpit just behind the normal one. The sliding canopy was removed, and both open cockpits were fitted with windscreens only. A few such machines were rebuilt in the USSR from single-seaters.

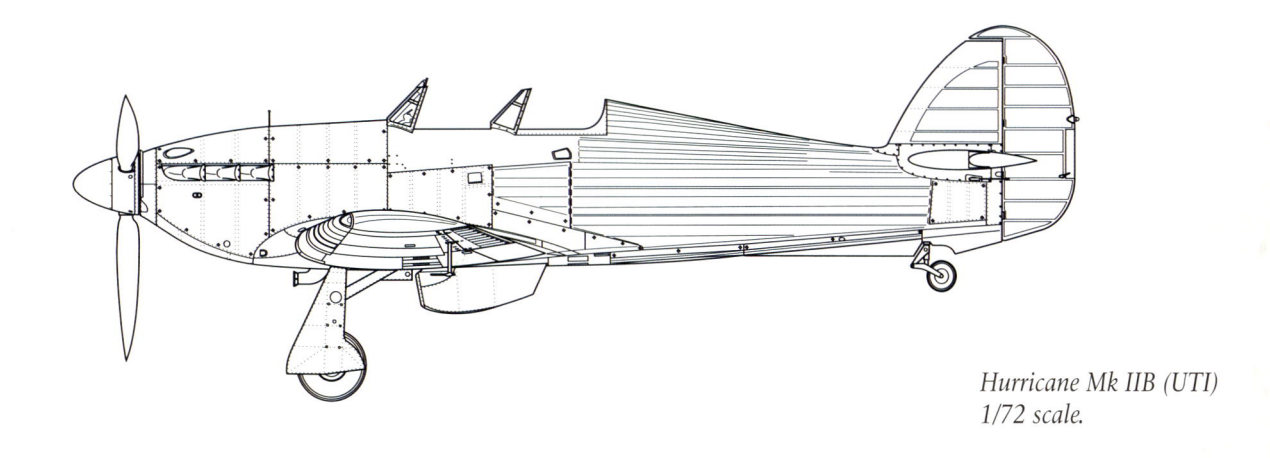

Hurricane Mk IIB (UTI) 1/72 scale.

Hurricane glider tug

Experiments with glider towing by a Hurricane were carried out in 1942 by the Red Army's experimental airborne troop unit in Saratov. This centre was established to research various methods of airborne landings. The centre was equipped with a few Mk IIC Hurricanes, which were used for towing A-7 gliders. The centre's Commanding Officer, A E Augul, performed a few flights with this combination, including some in inclement weather. Later the unit's Hurricane and A-7 glider combination was used in combat, and the British fighters were used by the centre until 1945. Some machines were also used for drogue target towing.

Other Soviet uses

The Soviets also tested Hurricanes fitted with skis (both fixed and retractable) for winter operations. Some fighters withdrawn from front-line units were converted to reconnaissance aircraft with an AFA-I/i or other (unknown) camera type installed just behind pilot's cockpit, in the same manner as in the British Tac R. Mk IIs. After the Great Patriotic War, Soviet Hurricanes were used for various other purposes, including at least one machine which was converted as a trainer for radio-operators.

Canada

Hurricane Mk X

In January 1939, the Canadian government agreed to the licensed production of Hurricanes at the Canadian Car and Foundry Co. in Montreal. A complete aircraft was sent from the UK to act as a pattern, along with a complete set of unassembled components and full drawings. These were initially referred to as Canadian s, but were quickly redesignated MkX to highlight their licence built status – some sources suggest that Mks II-IX had been earmarked for British-built variants. Production proceeded remarkably quickly despite little direct contact with Hawkers, and the first Canadian Hurricane flew less than a year after the production specification had been issued.

The first 40 Mk X Canadian Hurricanes were fitted with Merlin II or III engines and Watts or de Havilland airscrews supplied from the UK. They were usually known as Canadian Hurricane Mk I aircraft. Six were converted to Sea Hurricane Mk IA/B machines, while the next 320 machines of the second production order were fitted with eight Browning machine guns and Merlin 28 engines (a Merlin XX licence built by Packard).

All later Mk Xs were fitted with Hamilton Standard Hydromatic airscrews, distinctive due to their lack of spinner. Of the 340 aircraft of the second production order, 31 went to the Royal Canadian Air Force (RCAF) – RCAF Hurricane 1362, AG310, was used for tests of fixed skis. Twenty-five machines were converted to Sea Hurricanes and referred to as Mk IA or Mk IB, even though they were fitted with Merlin 28 engines. The third production order, 100 Mk Xs with Merlin 28 engines and eight machine guns, probably went entirely to the RAF, the fourth (of 50 aircraft) almost entirely to the USSR, and a few to the RCAF, and the fifth (150 aircraft) also to the RAF. Some of the RAF's machines went on to Africa, and others sent to the UK were re-fitted by 13 Maintenance Unit with Merlin XX engines and were re-classified as Mk IIB or Mk IIC as appropriate. (The total number of all "Mk X" Hurricanes amounted to 40 Canadian and 640 Mk X)

The Hurricane MkX helped facilitate the expansion and modernisation of the RCAF early in the war. The type was operated by squadrons in Canada for coastal defence and also by RCAF squadrons in Europe.

Hurricane Mk XI and XII

Aircraft of the Canadian sixth production batch, with Canadian rather than British equipment, were designated as Mk XI and Mk XII. The first (Mk XI) were powered with a Packard Merlin 28, and the remainder with Packard Merlin 29 engines, being designated Mk XII. 185 of them were armed with 12 machine guns (Mk XIB and XIIB), and 63 with four Hispano cannon (Mk XIC and XIIC). They went to RAF and RCAF squadrons, and, after conversion to Sea Hurricanes, also to FAA units. One machine of this batch was converted to a night fighter (NF Mk XIIC) with a Vokes tropical filter. The last batch of Canadian-built aircraft included 150 Mk XIIA Hurricanes, supplied in 1942 and 1943. They were equipped with Merlin 29 engines. A characteristic feature of Canadian Hurricanes used by Canada-based RCAF squadrons was that they usually flew without spinners.

Twelve aircraft of various marks (Mk I, Mk X, Mk XII) were fitted with fixed skis for winter operations.

British sources do not distinguish the models included in the 6th production order; it is quite possible that first 153 machines (JS219-JS371) were Mk XIs, the next 95 (JS374-JS468) Mk XIIs, and the cancelled machines JS372 and JS373 were a type of Mk XII "prototype". The number of manufactured aircraft (248) of the 6th production batch tally with the numbers above concerning the armament configuration (185 XIB or XIIB plus 63 XIC or XIIC). However, Canadian sources mention that the last Mk XIs were fitted with Merlin 29 engines and designated Mk XIB. Four machines of this production order were converted to Sea Hurricanes.

And, finally, the 7th production order of 150 Mk XII Hurricanes was designated (according to Canadian sources) Mk XIIA, and thus were probably armed with eight machine guns.

Unfortunately, the quantity of aircraft supplied to the RAF from the 6th and 7th orders remains unknown. It is certain that all 400 aircraft (including the two cancelled – see above) received RCAF serials (5376–5775), as well as RAF serials. Canadian sources claim that almost all served with the RCAF, being used as the equipment of 10 squadrons.

Canadian Hurricane production ended in 1943 after some 1,451 examples had come off the production lines.

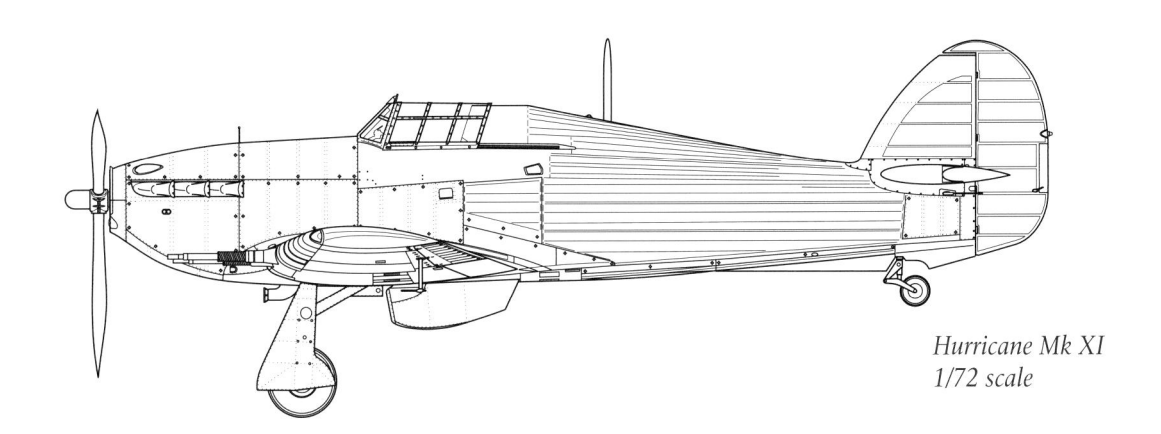

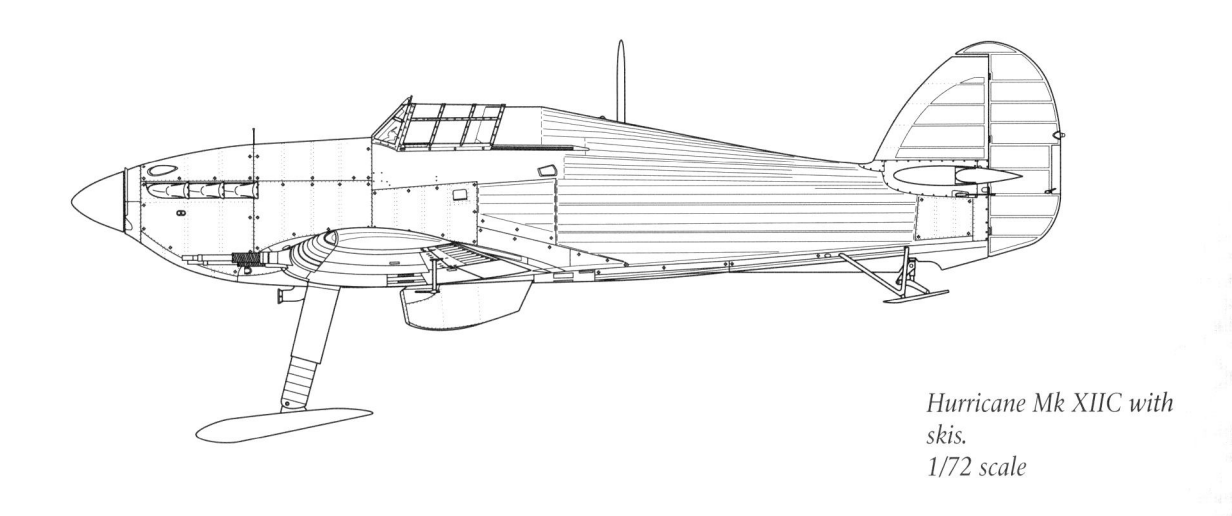

Hurricane Mk XI
1/72 scale

Hurricane Mk XIIC with skis.
1/72 scale

This 12 gun Canadian Hurricane, seen at Vancouver and photographed by a RCAF photographer shows that the outer blast tunes have been wrapped and covered with fabric patches. The light exhaust staining, stencil under the port wing and neat camouflage demarcation are all of interest, as well as clear details of the propeller hub. (Guy Walters Collection via Jerry Vernon)

Experimental versions & designs

There were a number of experimental versions of the Hurricane, some as prospective production types that were never taken forward, others testing a range of armament fits or different engines with a view to future developments, and still more modified as test-beds for other projects.

Cancelled production types

The Mk III was identical to the Mk IIC, but fitted with a US licence-built Merlin 28 engine. The Merlin 28 was the US version of the Merlin XX, and its use would be a solution to possible interruption in delivery of Merlin XXs. This turned out to be unnecessary, and the Mk III was never built.

The last proposed development of the Hurricane, a full ten years after Sydney Camm's initial "Fury Monoplane" proposals, was the Mk V. This was intended as a heavy ground attack aircraft for tropical climates, particularly Burma. The new Hurricane was developed from the V, but in keeping with its projected use in hot climates was to utilise the Merlin 32, which was boosted to over 1,700 hp at low level. In addition, the armoured radiator bath was deepened for greater cooling and the 3-bladed airscrew replaced with a 4-blade Rotol 5/4 unit. The prototype, KZ193, was initially tested with 2 Vickers "S" guns fitted in November 1943 at Boscombe Down, where impressive performance but difficult handling was noted. At "deck level" the Mk V was faster than a late model Mk I despite a 50% weight increase, but longitudinal and lateral stability were very poor in some circumstances. In an attempt to cure the stability problems, a 3-blade airscrew was fitted, but despite some improvement the Mk V was shelved. The Hurricane was clearly reaching the limit of its development potential, and obsolescence was approaching.

Experiments with armament fit for RAF Hurricanes

In specification F.37/35 issued at the beginning of 1936, the Air Ministry suggested an option to arm the fighter with four 20 mm Oerlikon cannon, instead of the eight machine guns. Camm replied to the Ministry's order on April 23rd with a modified Hurricane design. Calculations suggested that, with cannon installed, the maximum speed would drop to 260 mph (418 kph) at 13,000 ft (3,962 m), which was regarded as inadequate performance.

The test aircraft was intended to be V7360, but concerns over the fabric-covered wings caused the design to be rejected, and the Westland Whirlwind was chosen as the machine meeting the requirements of specification F.35/37.

Simultaneously with start of production of metal wings for Hurricanes, at the end of 1938 the Air Ministry ordered the experimental fitting of one machine with two Oerlikon cannon. For this purpose Hurricane L1750 was used, fitted with metal wings without armament, but with cannon pods under wings, which reduced the maximum speed to 300 mph (483 kph). It turned out that Oerlikon cannon were not suitable for installation in a fighter, as they were found to be insufficiently accurate, had a low rate of fire and required special ammunition only made by the cannon's manufacturer. The decision to abandon this type of cannon in favour of the same calibre Hispano was taken during the flight tests of L1750.

The subsequent fate of L1750 is very interesting. When war broke out the aircraft was stored at North Weald and was not "mobilised" until August 13th, 1940, when Flight Lieutenant Roddick L "Dick" Smith of 151 Sqn intercepted and shot down a Do 17 while flying L1750. This was probably the first British victory gained with the help of 20 mm cannon.

Sydney Camm responded to an Air Ministry request concerning Hispano cannon with the idea of arming a Hurricane with four such cannon. In July 1940, V7360, with metal wings and a battery of four 20 mm Hispano cannon, flew from Langley for the first time. The wings were taken from a crashed machine.

The aircraft went to Boscombe Down, where on August 13th, 1940, it was test flown by Sergeant "Sammy" Wroath. The power plant consisted of a Merlin II with a Rotol airscrew and the take-off weight amounted to 6,610 lb (2,998 kg). The maximum speed was 304 mph (489 kph) at 17,600 ft (5,365 m).

This prototype was transferred to 46 Sqn at Stapleford Tawney for operational tests. The machine was marked PO-B and on September 5th, 1940, Flight Lieutenant A C Rabagliati shot down a Messerschmitt Bf 109E while flying it.

V7360 was later rebuilt for the installation of four belt-fed Hispano cannon (instead of drum-fed) with a Chatellerault feed system, and this required a complete re-design of the gun bay and local internal wing structure.

In January 1940, Camm proposed improving the Hurricane's firepower by installing two additional .303 Browning machine guns in each outer wing, thus increasing their total number to twelve. One Hurricane Mk I was fitted with modified metal wings. However, due to the development of the Hurricane Mk II, this armament was introduced in production for the Mk IIB.

Hurricane Mk IV KZ706 was adapted for installation of two "Long Tom" rockets. The 500 lb (227 kg) rockets were mounted on long single rails and powered with three solid fuel rocket engines.

Photographs of the aircraft were taken in 1945 at Farnborough but without rockets fitted. There also seems to be no surviving information about the scope of the trials carried out.

Experiments with landing gear and auxiliary equipment

The Norway campaign in 1940 showed that on occasion it might be necessary to extend the range of the Hurricane. P3462 was modified at the Kingston factory for the installation of two 44 gal (200 l) tanks under the wings. The aircraft was test flown by Dick Rynell on May 7th, 1940. The results were utilised in later versions, which were fitted as standard for the installation of additional fuel tanks. This was especially useful for tropicalised aircraft, whose pilots usually flew long-range missions over the desert.

The next idea resulting from the Norway campaign's sudden requirements was the idea of a floatplane fighter, where floats would replace the wheeled gear. On April 26th, 1940, floats from a Blackburn Roc were transferred to Kingston and installed on a Hurricane. Test flights were to start in June, but due to the sudden end of the Norway campaign on June 10th, 1940, further work was abandoned.

Simultaneously with the floatplane developments, work was carried out on a ski-equipped version. For the same reasons this was abandoned, but later resumed after the start of licence production in Canada.

Hurricane L1696 was used as a test aircraft for slat-equipped wings. These additional high-lift wing devices were expected to facilitate take-off and landing, but were not applied to production-built aircraft. L1696 remained the only Hurricane thus equipped.

Alternative powerplants

In June 1939, Hurricane Mk I L1856 was fitted with the Rolls-Royce RM. 3S engine (later designated as Merlin VIII). The engine was just a standard Merlin III equipped with a two-speed supercharger and a de Havilland airscrew. The aircraft underwent standard ground testing and was test flown by Dick Reynell on July 7th, 1939.

The next experimental aircraft was the factory-owned G-AFKX (L1606), fitted with a Merlin XII engine. In this configuration the aircraft was test flown by K Seth-Smith on July 13th, 1939. The machine was later used as the test bed for the Rolls-Royce RM 4S (Merlin 45) engine with a Rotol airscrew.

A design for a Hurricane powered with a liquid-cooled 24-cylinder in-line horizontal-H engine, the Napier Dagger III, rated at 809 hp (595 kW) and armed with four Hispano cannon, was proposed as an alternative in case of problems with the supply of Merlin engines. It was not built.

Another back-up design anticipating potential issues with the Merlin was to be powered by an air-cooled 14-cylinder two-row radial Bristol Hercules engine rated at 1,375 hp (1,012 kW). This was also not built.

A third design of a Hurricane with an alternative to the Merlin was intended to be powered by a liquid-cooled 12-cylinder in-line Vee Rolls-Royce Griffon IIA engine rated at 1,720 hp (1,266 kW). This was intended as a dedicated ground attack machine, but the success of the Typhoon in this role rendered it unnecessary.

Increased visibility

There were at least two attempts, one unofficial and one official, to improve the visibility from the Hurricane's cockpit. Mk I P3221 was fitted by Squadron Leader A.H. Boyd of 145 Squadron with a new sliding hood, without framing but with teardrop-shaped bubbles on both sides, similar to those used in reconnaissance Spitfires, to increase rearward visibility. In 1942 Hurricane P3899 was selected to be fitted with a bubble canopy, requiring the top decking of the rear fuselage to be cut down, but in March 1943 the project was abandoned.

Unconventional proposals

An unusual experiment, for which there is no corroborating evidence, was in minesweeping. At the beginning of 1943 Hurricane KZ381 was supposedly fitted with an electromagnetic ring of 39.5 ft (12 m) diameter under the fuselage, fastened with brackets at the wingtips and rear fuselage. The machine was intended to sweep magnetic mines while flying low over the sea surface, causing them to explode after the aircraft had passed. The prototype was flown by Pamela Golan, an Air Transport Auxiliary (ATA) pilot, and she discovered that the encumbered Hurricane now stalled at 144 mph (231 kph). On April 18th she flew it from Hullavington, Wilts to Hatfield, Herts, where, together with other secret aircraft, it was shown to Churchill. The aircraft later returned to Hullavington, where the ring was removed.

Problematically, there is no official data on this and the only source was the pilot herself. According to her relations, there were records in the aircraft's log-book regarding test flights at the Arms & Armament Experimental Establishment (A&AEE), Telecommunications Research Establishment (TRE) and Royal Aircraft Establishment (RAE), which suggest that the aircraft was intensively tested. Official records do not mention Churchill's visit to Hatfield.

Some unusual solutions were also suggested to bring valuable fighters to besieged Malta in 1941. It was decided to test the idea of towing Hurricanes to the island. The project was developed by in-flight refuelling pioneers Flight Refuelling Ltd, and consisted of a Wellington bomber towing a fighter. When in range of the destination, the fighter would start its own engine and be released to land.

The Wellington was fitted with towing gear, and the Hurricane's (V7480) cockpit was equipped with a lever for tow-cable release. The steel cable of 590 ft (180 m) length was fastened to a triangular mounting under the fighter's fuselage just behind the cockpit. Two shorter cables ran from the plate to tow-hooks on the leading edge of each wing. Both aircraft took off with engines running, but connected by the slack cable. Having reached the desired cruise altitude, the fighter pilot switched off his engine and the fighter was towed as a glider. The angle of the cables (45°) was set so that that the airscrew arc fitted between them.

Testing was carried out at Staverton, Gloucestershire. During one flight, with Charles Barnard as the pilot, the tow cable did not release properly from one wing. The Wellington's crew was forced to release the cable, which was still attached to the Hurricane. Landing with the heavy cable trailing from the wing was a challenge, as it would touch the ground before the aircraft. Bernard was forced to land at high speed. Due to such problems and the substantial risk for both aircraft, plus the arrival of other solutions, the idea was abandoned.

A not-dissimilar idea to increase the range and short-field performance of the Hurricane was the "bi-mono" Hurricane. In 1941 W R Chown enlisted the help of a small firm called F. Hill & Sons (Hillson) to build a small single-seat aircraft called the "Bi-Mono". It was a low wing monoplane fitted with a detachable upper wing, which could be jettisoned in flight. The idea was that the aircraft had the advantages of a biplane during take-off (low wing loading, high lift) and of a monoplane (speed) during flight. Tests of the Bi-Mono were carried out in 1941 at Boscombe Down. In 1942 the Air Ministry commissioned the development of similar wing for the Hurricane. The intention was that this wing would contain an integral long-range fuel tank.

A wooden wing of the same shape as the Hurricane's was built, but without flaps or ailerons fitted. The wing was attached to the fighter with explosive bolts at the outer edge of the centre section, and the wing would descend by parachute. Tests were carried out with Hurricane L1884 between May 1943 and the summer of 1944 at Boscombe Down. One wing release in flight was undertaken, but the wing was never tested as a fuel tank. The aircraft was later scrapped.

Technology testbed

Hurricane Mk IIB Z3687 was used by Armstrong Whitworth for trials connected with development of the experimental A.W. 52 aircraft. This was a single-seat jet aircraft used as an aerodynamic test-model for a proposed larger jet bomber. The A.W. 52 was built as a flying wing with laminar-flow wing section. However, the company needed data about such a wing, and decided to research it using another airframe.

Hurricane Z3687 arrived at the Armstrong Whitworth plant in the latter half of 1944. Here the original centre section was fitted with outer wings of similar plan form to the Hurricane, but with a laminar flow wing section for nearly the entire length, only increasing in thickness in the area joining the centre section. The new wings were heavier by 322 lb (146 kg) than the standard ones. Sensors were installed on the upper and lower wing surfaces to measure the pressure distribution.

The aircraft was converted at the beginning of 1945, and on March 23rd Charles K Turner-Hughes, chief test pilot for Armstrong Whitworth, first flew it. On April 30th the aircraft went to Farnborough for further tests, which lasted until October. The results were not promising, but this was partially the fault of inadequately finished wing surfaces. The Hurricane returned to the workshops and it was much later, on April 18th, 1946, when it flew again. Tests lasted until November 1948 and the aircraft was then transferred to 19 MU, where was stored until April 9th, 1951, and finally scrapped.

HURRICANE Mk I – TECHNICAL DESCRIPTION

The Hawker Hurricane Mk I was a single-seat single-engine fighter aircraft of metal structure partially covered with fabric, fitted with retractable landing gear and enclosed cockpit.

The FUSELAGE was a metal framework made of four tubular longerons and metal crossbars braced with steel RAF wires. The entire fuselage was divided into three sections: a front section with engine mount, the central section with pilot's cockpit, and the rear section. The fuselage spine behind the cockpit was covered with fabric-lined plywood, and the sides of the central part of the fuselage and the engine were covered with sheet metal. The rear part was covered with doped fabric.

The front and the central part were separated by a firewall consisting of duralumin plates sandwiching an asbestos panel. Aft of the firewall was the reserve fuel tank. The framework in its central part was connected to the wing centre section structure forming one integral unit. The pilot's cockpit was situated above the centre section and behind the reserve fuel

A rare 1940 period shot of a Mk I Hurricane of 17 Sqn at dispersal. Note the Rotol propeller and integral rear view mirror. (Robert Gretzyngier)

tank, was covered with a two-part canopy consisting of a windscreen and a sliding hood. In the first production aircraft the windscreen had no armoured glass, but later aircraft were fitted with this feature. On the top of the windscreen was a rear-view mirror. A "break out" panel was fitted below the canopy on the starboard side, for emergency access use.

The cockpit was fitted with flight instruments and a metal pilot's seat with adjustable height. The main instruments were grouped on a vertical panel at the front of the cockpit, and the basic flight instruments were installed on a vibration insulated panel in the centre of the instrument panel.

Just behind the cockpit was the radio equipment, and in the fuselage spine two downward launch tubes for flares. On the spine behind the cockpit the antenna mast was mounted. Tropicalised aircraft were fitted with a container for food, water, mirror, signal cloth and signal pistol situated just behind the radio compartment.

The wing centre section, which formed one integral part together with the fuselage, was covered with duralumin skin; situated here were wheel bays, cooling system openings, radiator and radiator housing mounting, oil tank and fuel tanks. At the ends of the centre section were four attachment points for the outer wings. In aircraft from the first production series part of the centre section was covered with fabric.

The WING was of metal, two-spar structure with metal ribs and two auxiliary spars. It had tapered shape with rounded tips. The wing section was a modified Clark YH of 19% thickness (wing chord 8 ft 1 in /2.47m) at the wing root and Clark YH of 12.2% thickness (wing chord 4 ft /1.2 m) at the outer end of the mainplane. Dihedral angle was 3.5° (the centre section had 0° dihedral), wing incidence was 2°, and the sweep angle 5°6'.

The first few hundred production machines had wings covered with

Hawker built Mk I P3886, here seen undergoing some servicing, was issued to 601 Sqn, Exeter in October 1940 before going onto 1 Sqn at Kenley in 1941 after an accident. (Robert Gretzyngier)

Hurricane Mk IIC of 309 (Polish) Sqn. (Stratus coll.)

fabric, the remaining ones with all-metal stressed-skin construction skin. The fabric-cover type wings were replaced as soon as possible with the all-metal wings. The introduction of metal skin also led to repositioning of the landing lights and armament. On the fabric covered wing, the fabric skin strips were laid over the structure at a 45° angle in relation to the wing chord. The metal skin was riveted to ribs and spars with round-head rivets. The wings housed the gun compartments and ammunition containers.

The wings were fitted with ailerons and hydraulically operated flaps. The ailerons, of metal structure, were covered with fabric, and the flaps were of all-metal structure. The ailerons of 20.4 sq ft (1.895 m^2) area could be deflected by 22° upward and 21° downward; they were mounted with hinges to the rear spar. The flaps were attached to the wing in the same way; their area amounted to 25.12 sq ft (2.333 m^2) and the maximum deflection angle was 80°.

The TAIL UNIT consisted of a fin with rudder and a horizontal tailplane with elevators. They were of metal structure with ribs and spars, and were covered with fabric. The span of the elevator unit was 11 ft (3.353 m) and its mean geometrical chord was 4 ft 2in (1.28 m). The horizontal tailplane area was 19.60 sq ft (1.821 m^2) and the elevator area 13.45–13.70 sq ft (1.250–1.273 m^2). The elevator deflection angle was 27° upward and 20° downward. The elevators were fitted with flight-adjustable trim tabs and smaller ground-adjustable trim plates protruding outside the elevator contour. Some machines were fitted with trim plates on the right elevator only.

The fin of similar structure had an area of 8.81 sq ft (0.819 m^2) and the rudder of 12.68 sq ft (1.178 m^2) in early versions without the ventral fin, and of 13.06 sq ft (1.213 m^2) in fin-fitted aircraft. The rudder deflection angle was 28° in both directions.

The main UNDERCARRIAGE was hydraulically retracted in flight. Main wheels fitted with oleo-pneumatic shock absorbers were retracted into the centre section and covered with doors. The first production aircraft were fitted with a retractable tailwheel, but later machines had a fixed one.

The wheel track was 7 ft 10 in (2.388m) and the wheels were fitted with pneumatic brakes. Tyre pressure were 0.41–0.45lb/in (290–317kPa) for main wheels and 0.39–0.52lb/in (276–372kPa) for the tailwheel.

The POWERPLANT consisted of a 12-cylinder in-line liquid-cooled Rolls-Royce Merlin engine. First batches were equipped with a Merlin II engine driving a wooden two-blade Watts Z 38 airscrew of 10ft 8in (3.249m) diameter or a metal three-blade two-position de Havilland airscrew of 11 ft (3.352m) diameter. From September 1939 Hurricane Mk Is were fitted with a Merlin III engine, which was adapted for various types of de Havilland airscrews (usually 5/32) or for a three-blade variable-pitch Rotol RX5/2 airscrew of 10 ft 9 in (3.277m) diameter with blades made of mechanically processed wood.

Both engines had identical parameters. Take-off output was 890 hp (664 kW) with 87-octane fuel and 1,195 hp (954 kW) with 100-octane fuel, at 2,850 rpm. The maximum power was 1,030 hp (891 kW) with 87-octane fuel at 16,240 ft (4,950m) and 1,270 hp (891 kW) with 100-octane fuel at 7,910 ft/2,410 m. The weight of a dry engine was 624 kg (1,376 lb). Fuel consumption at economic power was 23 gal (105 l) per hour and at combat power 89gal (405 l) per hour.

The Merlin II/III installed in Hurricanes was fitted with a reduction gear of 0.477:1 reduction ratio, the Merlin being classed as a "right hand tractor", the propeller rotating clockwise viewed from aft. The coolant, ethylene glycol, was contained in a tank fastened to the firewall just in front of the cockpit. The radiator was mounted under the fuselage and the airflow through it was adjusted by a exit flap operated manually by the pilot. The engine was fitted with an electric starter, but could be also started manually with help of two cranks, with connectors situated on the engine cowling sides. The Merlin II/III was fitted with a single-speed mechanical supercharger.

Aircraft operating in tropical and dusty conditions were fitted with special Vokes Multi V filter type installed on the carburettor air inlet. The pilot could direct the air passed through the filter or bypass it.

The FUEL SYSTEM consisted of two centre-section mounted main tanks of 34.5 gal (157 l) capacity each covered with self-sealing layer, and a reserve tank of 28 gal (127 l) installed in the fuselage in front of the cockpit.

Some machines were fitted with a system allowing installation of two 44 gal (200 l) tanks under the wings.

The OIL SYSTEM consisted of a main tank of 10.5 gal (47.7 l) capacity mounted in the front part of the left wing root, an additional 4 gal (18 l) tank in the fuselage, and an oil pump. Oil pressure was 73lb/in (5 atm).

The HYDRAULIC SYSTEM was used for retracting and lowering the undercarriage and for actuation of flaps. The first aircraft were equipped with a manual hydraulic pump, later ones with one mechanically-driven (from the engine).

The PNEUMATIC SYSTEM consisted of an engine-driven compressor. The system supplied compressed air for wheel brakes, gun trigger and camera gun. System pressure was 2.07 MPa.

The ELECTRICAL SYSTEM of DC type (12 V) consisted of a 500 W generator and a 40 Ah battery situated behind the pilot's seat. The system supplied power to the lighting system, reflector gunsight, camera gun (G.42B only), instruments, radio and engine starter. From 1941 the system also powered electrically heated pilot's gloves and boots.

The OXYGEN SYSTEM consisted of tanks situated under the pilot's seat.

The DE-ICING SYSTEM for the windscreen consisted of a 0.55 gal (2.5 l) tank and a manual pump.

The RADIO EQUIPMENT consisted of a short-wave transceiver T.R. 9B or D with a wire antenna spread between the aerial mast and the fin. From March 1940 an ultrashort-wave transceiver T.R. 1133 was fitted.

The ARMAMENT consisted of eight .303 (7.7 mm) Browning Mk II machine guns, firing 1,200 rounds per min, mounted in fours in the wings. Ammunition supply for individual guns was 338 rounds for the guns closest to the fuselage, 324 for the next one, and 338 for the remaining two. An alternative arrangement was 370, 490, 380 and 395 rounds, working from the fuselage to the wingtip. The harmonisation of the guns was set to 200 – 300 yards (180-275 m). A three-second salvo weighed 8 lb (3.63 kg). The blast tubes were covered on the ground with rectangular pieces of red doped fabric.

The gun trigger was situated on the control stick. First aircraft were fitted with a ring and bead gunsight, later ones with a G.M.2 reflector gunsight. Additionally, in the right wing root a G.22A or B camera gun (later G.42B or G.45) was installed. To avoid freezing at altitude they were heated with warm air supplied from the radiator.

HURRICANE Mk IIC – TECHNICAL DESCRIPTION

(Variations from the Mk I Specifications only)

The POWERPLANT consisted of a 12-cylinder in-line liquid-cooled Rolls-Royce Merlin XX engine fitted with a single-stage, mechanical two-speed supercharger. The engine drove a three-blade Rotol RS5/2 or RS5/3 airscrew of 11 ft 3 in (3.429 m). The take-off output was 1,319 hp (984 kW), 1,460 hp (1,090 kW) at 6,250 ft (1,905 m) and 1,435 hp (1,070 kW) at 11,000 ft (3,353 m), all at 3,000 rpm. Only 100-octane fuel was used, which was consumed at economy power at 30 gal (136 l) /h and at combat power 115 gal (523 l) /h. The weight of a dry engine was 1,446 lb (656 kg).

The aircraft of late production batches were fitted with Merlin 24 engines rated at 1,610 hp (1,201 kW) take-off power, 1,630 hp (1,215 kW) at 2,500 ft (760 m) and 1,510 hp (1,126 kW) at 9,252 ft (2,820m).

The FUEL SYSTEM was identical to the Mk I, but besides 44 gal (200 l) under-wing tanks, 45 gal (205 l) or 90 gal (409 l) tanks could be fitted.

The ARMAMENT consisted of four 20 mm Hispano Mk I cannon in the wings, with 91 rounds per cannon.

HURRICANE Mk IV – TECHNICAL DESCRIPTION

(Further variations from the Mk II Specifications only)

The POWERPLANT consisted of a 12-cylinder in-line liquid-cooled Rolls-Royce Merlin 24, 27 or 32 engine fitted with a single-stage, mechanical two-speed supercharger offering 1,610 hp (1,201 kW) take-off power, 1,630 hp (1,215 kW) at 2,500 ft (760 m) and 1,510 hp (1,126 kW) at 9,252 ft (2,820m). The engine drove a three-blade Rotol RS 5/11 airscrew of 11 ft 3 in (3.429 m).

The ARMAMENT consisted of two wing-mounted .303in Browning machine guns, two 250 lb or 500 lb (113,4 kg, 226,8 kg) bombs or Small Bomb Containers (SBC) with fragmentation bombs, two Vickers "S" 40mm cannon, or eight 60lb rocket projectiles. In the case of the latter, blast plates needed to be fitted below the wings. Additional fuel tanks of various capacities could be fitted in place of wing armament. External armour was fitted to the radiator bath.

A Volkes filter equipped Hurricane lies wrecked and abandoned. (Stratus coll.)

Type	Mk I Watts	Mk I Rotol	Mk II Series 2	Mk IIB
Dimensions				
Span	40 ft (12.9 m)	40 ft (12.9 m)	40 ft (12.9 m)	40 ft (12.9 m)
Length	31 ft 5 in (9.58[1] m)	31 ft 5 in (9.58[1] m)	32 ft (9.75 m)	32 ft (9.75 m)
height	13 ft (3.98 m)	13 ft 3 in (4.04 m)	13 ft 3 in (4.04 m)	13 ft 3 in (4.04 m)
wing area	257.6 sq ft 23.93 m²	257.6 sq ft 23.93 m²	257.6 sq ft 23.93 m²	257.6 sq ft 23.93 m²
Weights take-off	6217 lb 2,820 kg	6446 lb 2,924 kg		7233 lb 3,281 kg
Weights empty	5238 lb 2,376[2] kg	4674 lb 2,120 kg	5150 lb 2,336 kg	5640 lb 2,558 kg
Weights Maximum	7490 lb 3,397[3]	8050 lb 3,651 kg	8250 lb 5,330 kg	
Performance				
max. speed at sea level	258 mph 415 kph	280 mph 451 kph	272 mph 438 kph	256 mph 412 kph
max. speed	305 mph 491 kph	324 mph 521 kph	342 mph 550 kph	330 mph 531 kph
at	17000 ft 5,180 m	17800 ft 5,425 m	17500 ft 5,330 m	17800 ft 5,425 m
climb to 20,000 ft	11.7 min	9.8 min	8.6 min	8.9 min
ceiling	33400 ft 10,180 m	34200 ft 10,424 m	36300 ft 11,064 m	36000 ft 10,970 m
range	440 miles 708 km	425 miles 684 km	469 miles 756 km	469 miles 756 km
max. range w/add. tanks	899 miles 1,448 km	951 – 1087 miles 1,530 – 1,750 km	939 – 1081 miles 1,512 – 1,740 km	

Type	Mk II C	Mk II D Trop	Sea Hurricane Mk IIC	Mk IV
Dimensions				
Span	40 ft (12.9 m)	40 ft (12.9 m)	40 ft (12.9 m)	40 ft (12.9 m)
Length	32 ft (9.75 m)	32 ft (9.75 m)	32 ft (9.75 m)	32 ft (9.75 m)

height		13 ft 3 in (4.04 m)	13 ft 3 in (4.04 m)	13 ft 3 in (4.04 m)	13 ft 3 in (4.04 m)
wing area		257.6 sq ft 23.93 m²	257.6 sq ft 23.93 m²	257.6 sq ft 23.93 m²	257.6 sq ft 23.93 m²
Weights	take-off	7544lb 3,422 kg	7848lb 3,560 kg	7617lb 3,455 kg	8333lb 3,780 kg
	empty	5800lb 2,630 kg	6722lb 3,049 kg	6931lb 2,899 kg	7207lb 3,269 kg
	Maximum	8040lb 3,647 kg	8540lb 3,874 kg	7800lb 3,538 kg	8510lb 3,860 kg
Performance					
max. speed at sea level		260 mph 418 kph		260 mph 418 kph	293 mph 471[4] kph
max. speed		329 mph 529 kph	320 mph 515 kph	317 mph 510 kph	314 mph 505 kph
at		17800 ft 5,425 m		17500 ft 5,330 m	13500 ft 4115 m
climb to 20,000 ft		9.1 min	12.4 min	8.1 min	9.3 min
ceiling		35600 ft 10,850 m	32100 ft 9,784 m	31700 ft 9,660 m	36000 ft 10970 m
range		460 miles 740 km	420 miles 676 km	452 miles 727 km	430 miles 692 km
max. range w/add. tanks		920 – 1086 miles 1,480 – 1,748 km	900 – 995 miles 1,450 – 1,601 km	907 – 1062 miles 1,460 – 1,710 km	910 miles 1,464[5] km

Notes:
1) – after re-calculation from Imperial (31ft 5 in), which is only a rough value. The value is given as the same for all Mk Is regardless of spinner type.
2) – without pilot, fuel and ammo, but with full equipment
3) – tropicalised version.
4) – at 2130 m/6990 ft.
5) – for ferry flight, w/o cannon.

General remarks:
Installation of a tropical filter caused:
reduction of max. speed by 30 – 42 mph (48-68 kph) **for Mk I** and 7 – 8 mph (11–13 kph) **for Mk II**;
reduction of climb rate by 5 – 6 ft/s (1.6-1.8 m/s) **for Mk I** and 2 – 4 ft/s (0.6-1.3 m/s) **for Mk II**;
reduction of range by 45 miles (72 km) **for Mk I**, 28-34 miles (45-55 km) **for Mk II A/B/C**, 16 miles (26 km) **for Mk IID**, 37 miles (60 km)

for Sea Hurricane Mk IIC;
reduction of ceiling by 4500 ft (1370 m) **for Mk I** and 1200 ft (370 m) **for Mk IIA**.
Additional fuel tanks 2x45 gal (205 l) reduced speed by 43 – 54 mph (69-87 kph) **for Mk IIB**.
Additional fuel tanks 2x90gal (409 l) reduced speed by 61 – 85 mph (98-136 kph) **for Mk IIB**.
Two 250 lb (113 kg) bombs reduced speed by 34 – 43 mph (56-69 kph) and climb rate by 2 – 5 ft/s (0.6-1.5 m/s) **for Mk IIB**.
Rockets reduced speed by 25 – 36 mph (40-58 kph) and climb rate by 13 – 14 ft/s (3.9-4.3 m/s) **for Mk IIA**.

In Detail Fuselage

Above: A good view of LF363 showing the texture and wear of the fuselage. (Robin Rawle)

Below: Port, front part of the fuselage of the Hurricane Mk I. (Dariusz Karnas)

Above: Starboard side of the Hurricane from the rear. The fuselage construction is visible. (Dariusz Karnas)

Below: An almost direct side-on view, amply illustrating the elusive nose and spine shapes, and many of the details. (Rob Leigh)

77

Port side of the Mk IIC LF738 at RAF Cosford. (Stratus coll.)

Rear starboard side of the Hurricane Mk I (HC-452) of Keski-Suomen Ilmailumuseo – Tikkakoski, Finland. (Martti Kujansuu)

Port side, central part of the fuselage, pilot's entry handles are visible. Hurricane Mk XII B (Can.). (James Kightly)

Front port side of the fuselage. Sea Hurricane Mk IB Z7015.

The fuselage wooden structure before covering.
(All photos James Kightly)

Hurricane Mk XII B in flight with the undercarriage down.

79

The starboard side of the Hurricane with the engine cowlings removed.

Rear upper part of the fuselage with wooden stringers visible.
(Both photos James Kightly)

Fuselage framework with wing spars attached. (Stratus coll.)

Rear, starboard side of the fuselage with tail removed. (Both James Kightly)

Upper fuselage wooden formers with stringers attached

Above: Fuselage framework with centre wing section attached.
Left: Fuselage framework. (Both Stratus coll.)
Bottom: Fuselage framework with engine mounts. Note also wooden formers and stringers in the rear part of the fuselage. (Steve Petterson)

81

Upper view of the Hurricane with skin removed. Details of the fuselage and tail are visible. (Steve Patterson)

Right and bottom: Two photos of the port side, centre section of the fuselage, Hurricane Mk I. (Martti Kujansuu)

Below: Extended foot-rest. Operation of the foot-rest automatically opens the entry handle which is visible in the photo on the right (in closed position). (Stratus coll.)

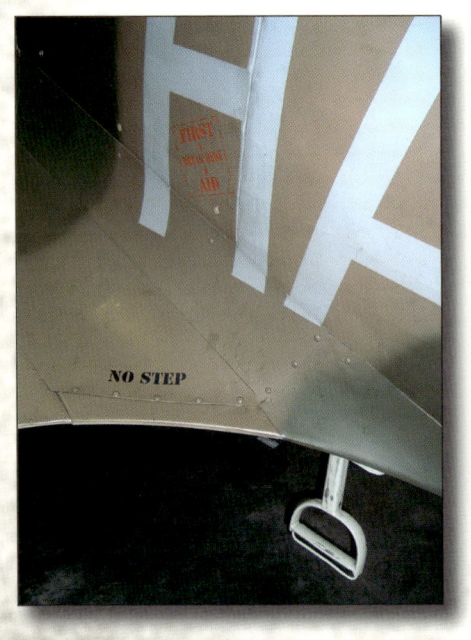

Lower part of the fuselage of the Sea Hurricane Mk I. Carburettor and radiator air intakes are visible. (Stratus col.)

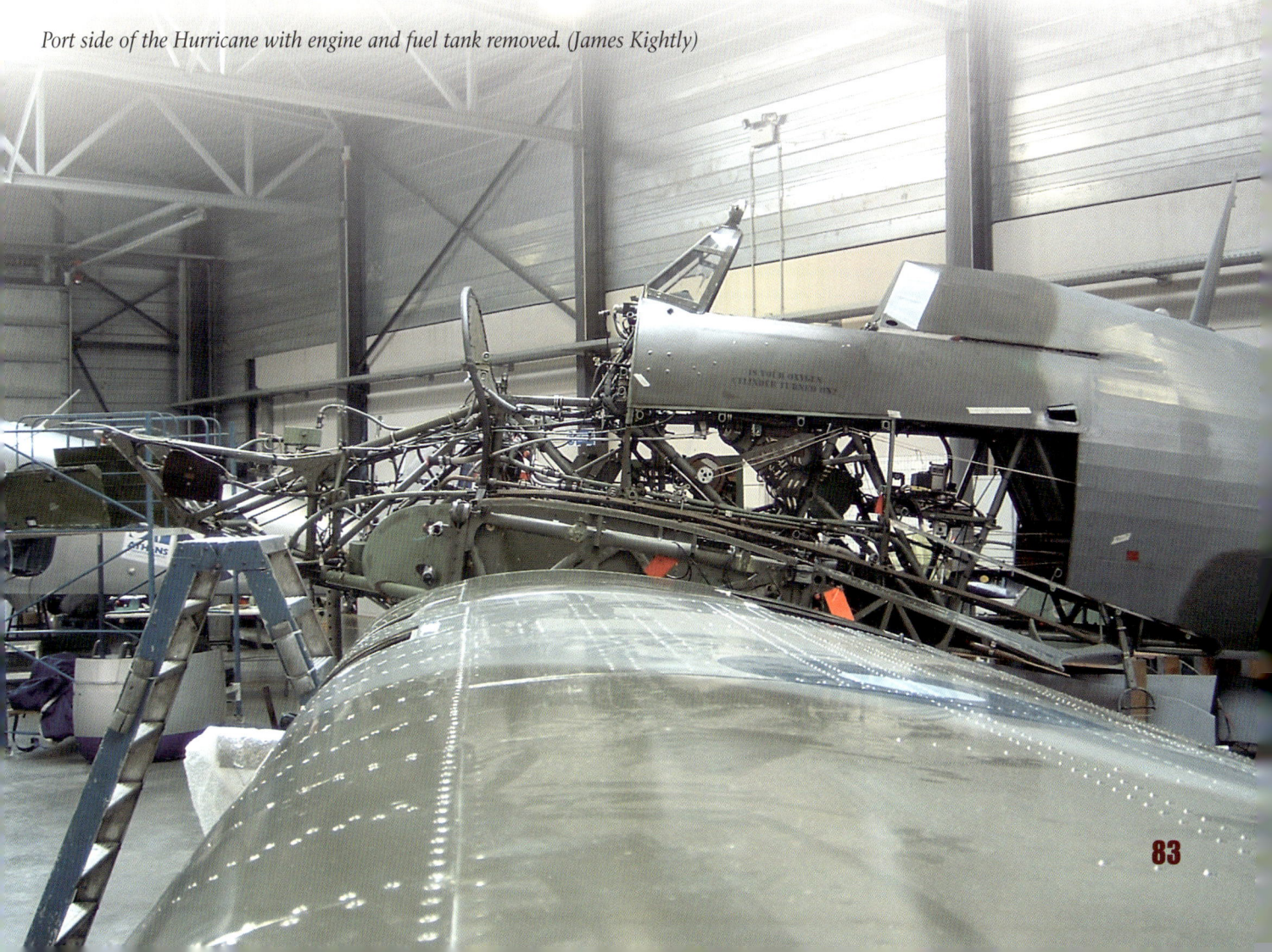

Port side of the Hurricane with engine and fuel tank removed. (James Kightly)

Above and right: Two photos of the cockpit entry handle in the open position.

Aerial mast, later version.

The front of the wing to fuselage fairing on the starboard side.
(All photos Stratus coll.)

84

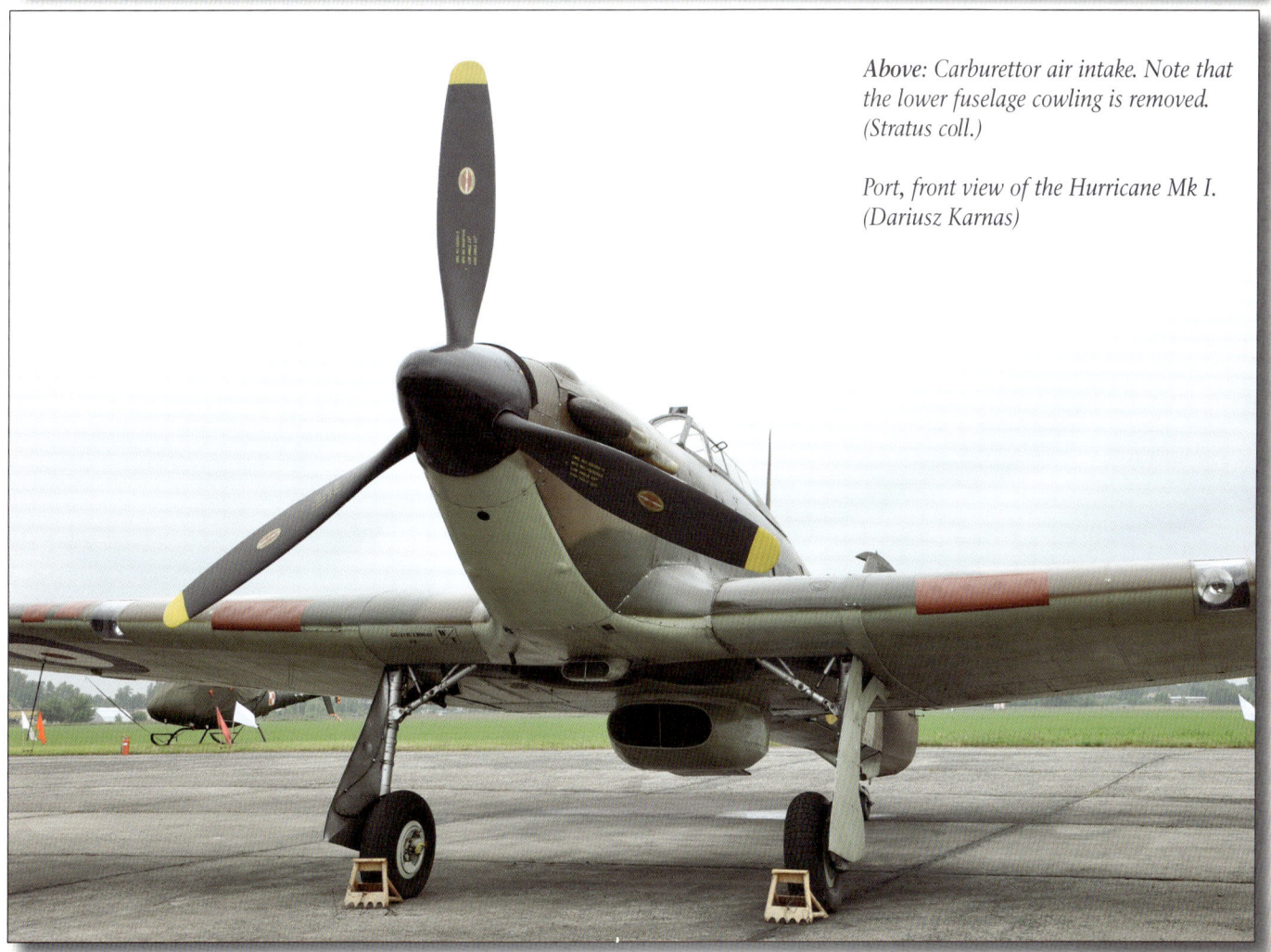

Above: Carburettor air intake. Note that the lower fuselage cowling is removed. (Stratus coll.)

Port, front view of the Hurricane Mk I. (Dariusz Karnas)

Above: Wing-fuselage fillet on the port side, Hurricane Mk I. (Martti Kujansuu)

Right: Port, 3/4 front view of the Hurricane Mk II. (Dariusz Karnas)

Details of the fuselage panels dzuses. (Dariusz Karnas)

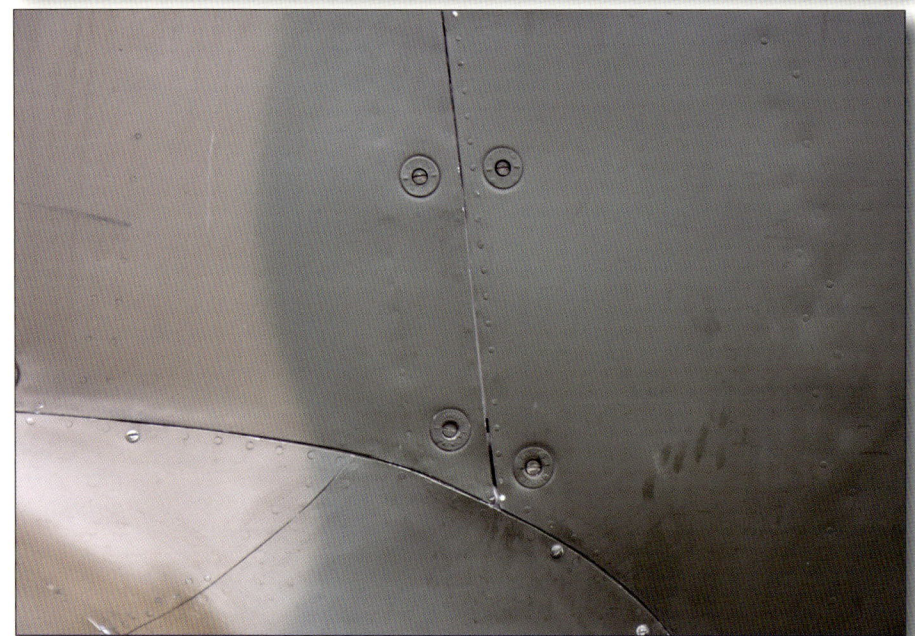

Wing-fuselage fillet from the rear. (Dariusz Karnas)

Top: *Two photos of the extended foot-rest (Stratus and Martti Kujansuu)*

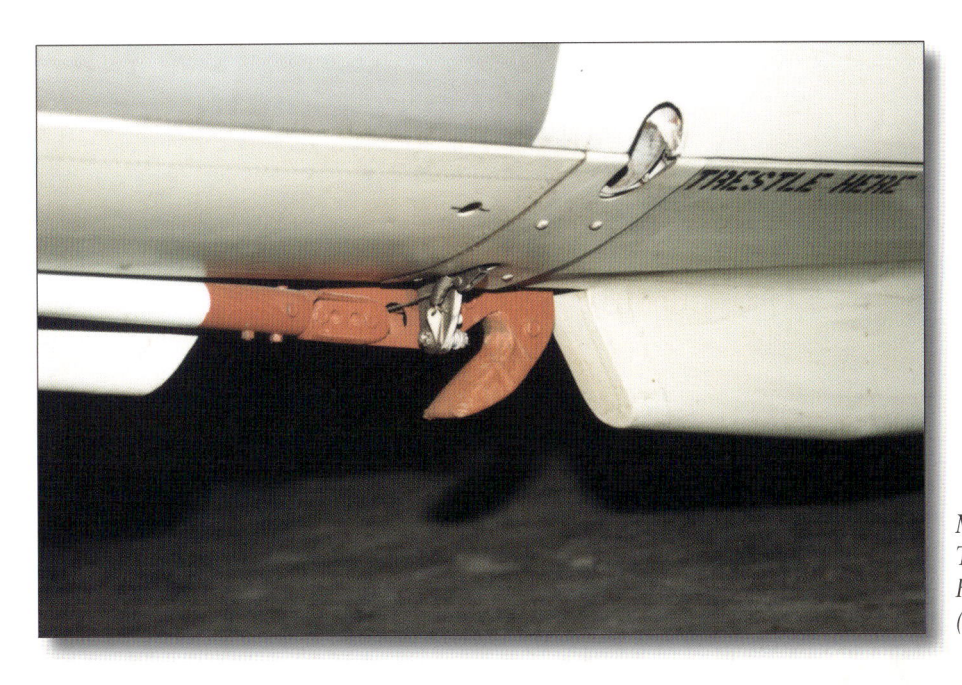

Middle & bottom:
Two photos of the arrestor hook at Sea Hurricane.
(Stratus coll.)

87

Canopy

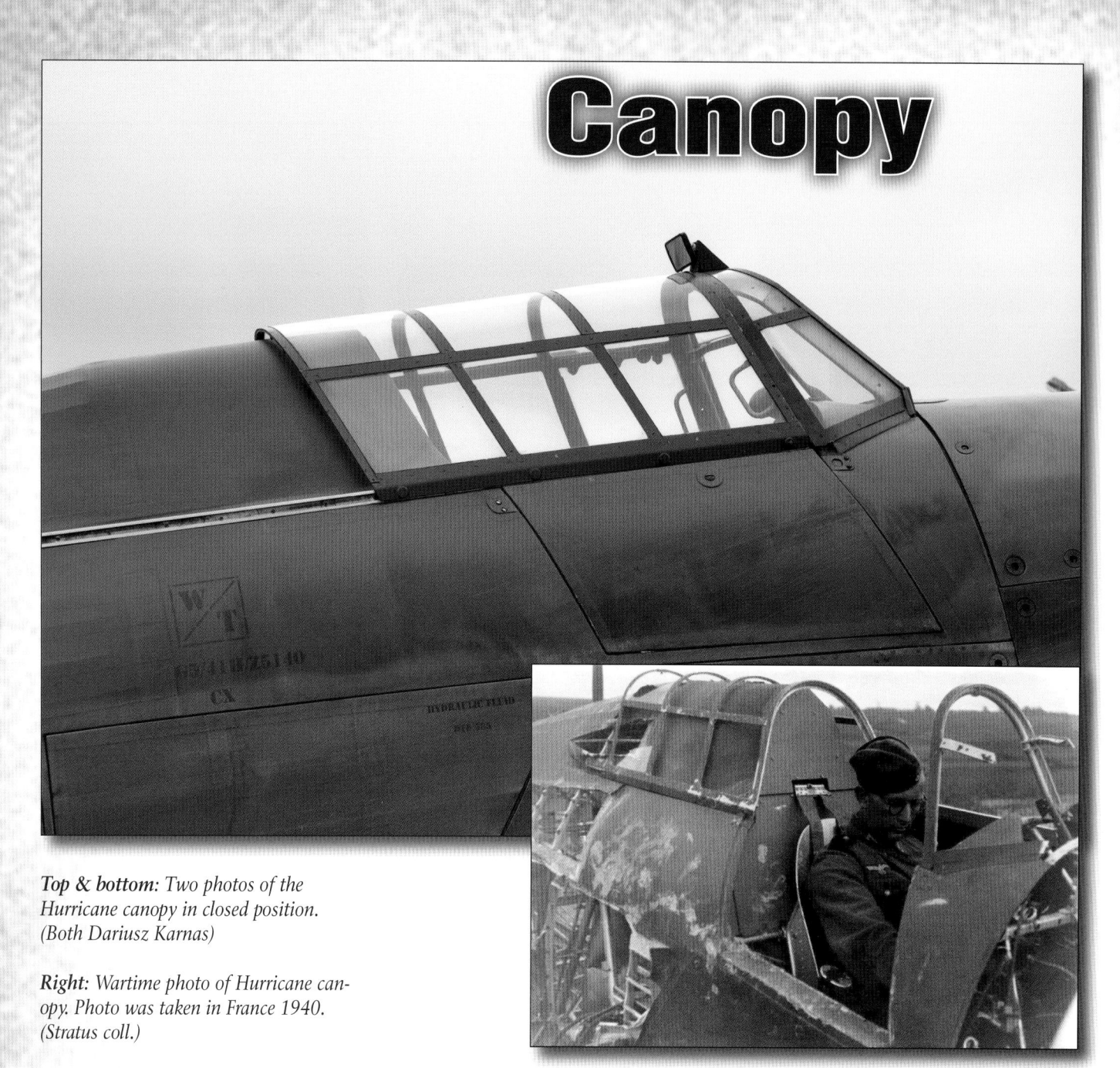

Top & bottom: Two photos of the Hurricane canopy in closed position. (Both Dariusz Karnas)

Right: Wartime photo of Hurricane canopy. Photo was taken in France 1940. (Stratus coll.)

88

Port side of the canopy in the closed position. Windscreen armoured glass is visible. (Dariusz Karnas)

Two photos of windscreen framing and rear-view mirror. (Both Stratus coll.)

Above: *Cockpit canopy slid back. (Stratus coll)*
Right: *Starboard side of the windscreen. (Dariusz Karnas)*

Rear view of the canopy slid back. Note the gap between canopy and fuselage. (Stratus coll.)

*Two photos of the canopy. Rails are well visible in the bottom photo.
(Both Dariusz Karnas)*

91

Cockpit

Instrument panel and the control column. Note the gun/cannon trigger in the upper part of the grip on the port side. The lever in the middle of the grip operates the main wheel brakes.

GM2 gun sight, as mounted on Sea Hurricane.
(Both Stratus coll.)

GM2 gun sight from the left.

Compass installed below the instrument panel.

Close-up view of the control column, heel boards and undercarriage/flaps lever. (All photos Stratus coll.)

KEY TO FIG. 2
32. Engine starter pushbutton
33. Booster coil pushbutton
34. Boost control cut-out
35. Oxygen regulator
36. Power failure warning light
37. Cockpit ventilator
38. Undercarriage indicator ON-OFF switch
39. Undercarriage indicator change-over switch
40. R.P. selector switch
41. Undercarriage indicator
42. Instrument flying panel.
43. Reflector sight spare lamps
44. Engine speed indicator
45. Reflector sight switch
46. Cockpit ventilator
47. Boost gauge
48. Fuel contents gauge selector switch
49. Fuel contents gauge
50. Fuel pressure warning light
51. Radiator temperature gauge
52. Beam approach master switch
53. Oil temperature gauge
54. Oil pressure gauge
55. Camera gun switch
56. Navigation lights switch
57. Pressure head heater switch
58. Ignition switches

KEY TO FIG. 1
11. Cannon master switch
12. Compass light dimmer switch
13. Cockpit light
14. Cockpit light dimmer switch
15. Landing lamp switch
16. Friction adjuster
17. Supercharger control
18. Fuel cock control
(continued at page 95)

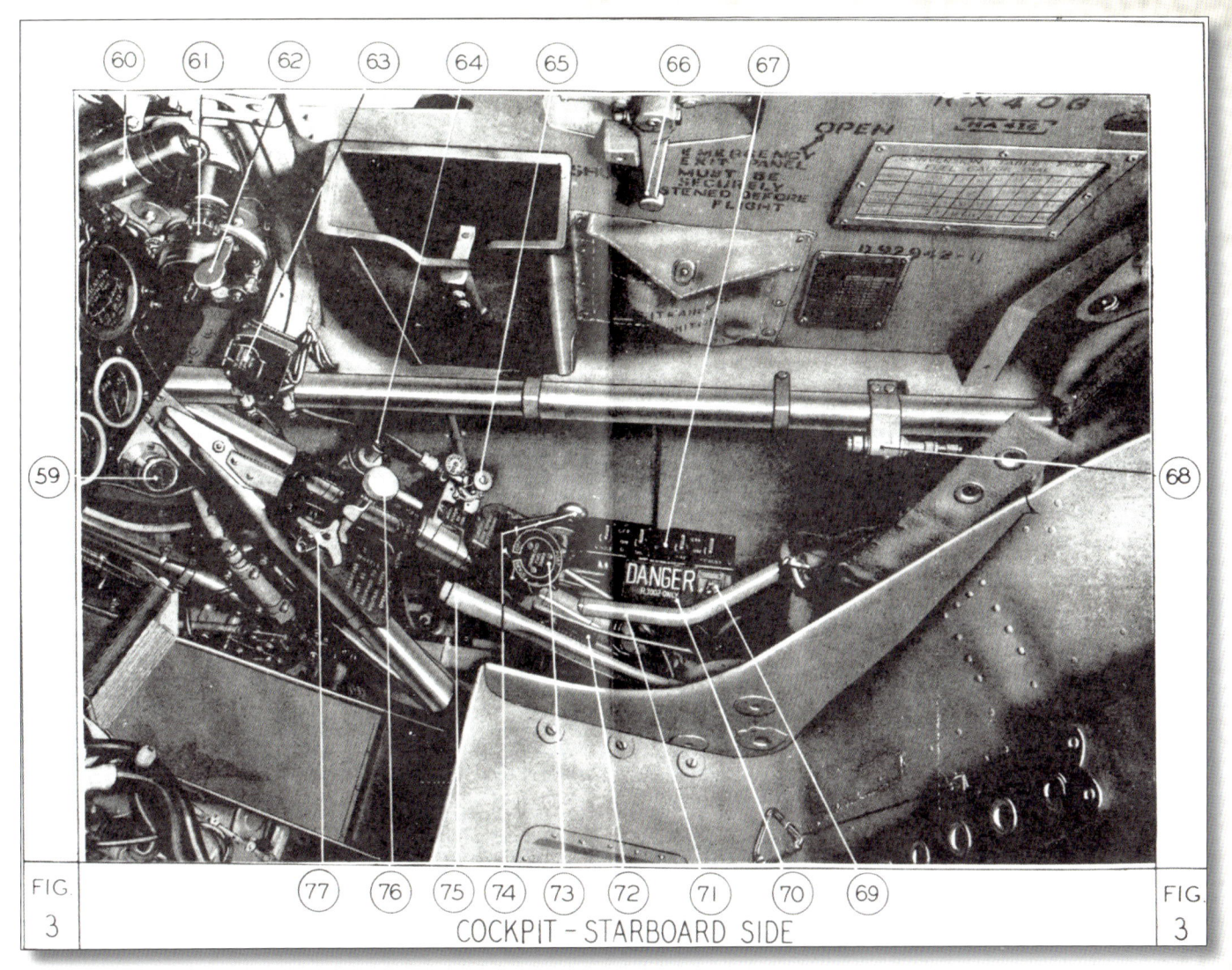

COCKPIT – STARBOARD SIDE

KEY TO FIG. 3
59. Cylinder priming pump
60. Cockpit light
61. Cockpit light dimmer switch
62. Signalling switch box
63. Flare jettison pushbutton
64. Slow-running cut-out
65. Windscreen de-icing pump
66. Emergency exit panel jettison lever
67. Bomb fusing and selector switches
68. Sutton harness release
69. I.F.F. master switch
70. I.F.F. pushbuttons
71. Hydraulic handpump
72. Flap indicator
73. Drop tank fuel cock control
74. Drop tank jettison control
75. Seat adjustment lever
76. Undercarriage and flap selector lever
77. Undercarriage selector safety catch

Below: *Left side of the instrument panel. (Stratus coll.)*

19. R.T.9D contactor switch
20. Radio contactor
21. Undercarriage emergency release lever
22. Fuel tank pressurising control
23. Rudder trimming tab control
24. Elevator trimming tab control
25. IFF device selector lever
26. Radiator flap control lever
27. Heated clothing socket
28. Cannon cocking lever
29. Microphone/telephone socket
30. Hood catch control
31. Voltmeter

GALLONS FUEL
TAIL ON GROUND
NORMAL FLIGHT
PORT
CENTRE
STBD
PUSH FOR READING
FUEL GAUGE SELECTOR
FUEL
OIL
BOOST
OFF
REFLECTOR SIGHT
CLIMB
THOUSAND FEET MIN
DESCENT
SIDE SLIP
TURN
L
R
ARTIFICIAL HORIZON
DIRECTION INDICATOR
ALT
UNDERCARRIAGE
UP
DOWN
DAY
NIGHT
12 VOLT
RED INDICATES WHEEL LOCKED UP GREEN INDICATES WHEEL LOCKED DOWN
SWITCH ON GREEN LAMP BEFORE FLYING SWITCH OFF GREEN LAMP AFTER FLYING
BUZZER WARNING WHEELS NOT LOCKED DOWN
OIL CAUSES EXPLOSIONS. DO NOT USE IT
OXYGEN REGULATOR MARK VIII C
OXYGEN SUPPLY AVAILABLE
FULL
EMPTY
DELIVERY
ALT. THOUSAND OF FEET
EMERGENCY
EMERGENCY USE ONLY
AUTOM BOOST CUT OUT CONTROL
PULL AND TURN TO LOCK BOOST
MAGNETO
Nº1 ON
Nº2 ON
STARTING
BOOSTER COIL
PUSH
PRESSURE HEAD HEAT
NAVIGATION LIGHTS
CINE CAMERA

Hawker Hurricane Mk I Instruments Panel:

1. Airspeed indicator
2. Artificial horizon
3. Rate of climb indicator (Variometer)
4. Altimeter
5. Direction indicator
6. Adjusting knob for direction indicator
7. Turning indicator
8. Change over switch for undercarriage position visual indicator
9. Undercarriage position visual indicator
10. Compass correction card holder
11. Oxygen flow indicator
12. Oxygen supply indicator
13. Oxygen regulator control valve
14. Automatic boost cut-out control
15. Engine starter push button
16. Booster coil push button
17. Main magneto switchesh
18. Instrument switches;
    – pressure head heater switch
    – navigation lamps switch
    – cine camera switch
19. Tachometer
20. Reflector sight lamp switch
21. Boost pressure gauge
22. Fuel contents gauge selector switch
23. Oil pressure gauge
24. Fuel pressure gauge
25. Fuel contents gauge
26. Oil temperature gauge
27. Radiator temperature gauge
28. Starting magneto switch

Drawings by Dariusz Karnas.

Right side of the instrument panel. Engine control instruments are visible. (Stratus coll.)

97

Left cockpit wall. The elevator trim wheel, is in the centre.
(All photos Stratus coll.)

Port side of the cockpit. The throttle and propeller pitch levers are visible.

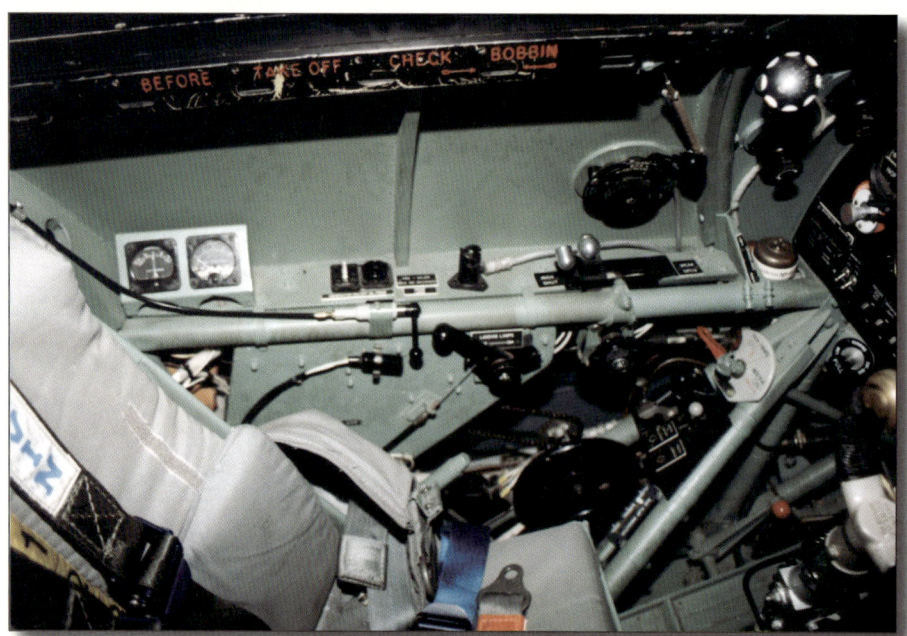

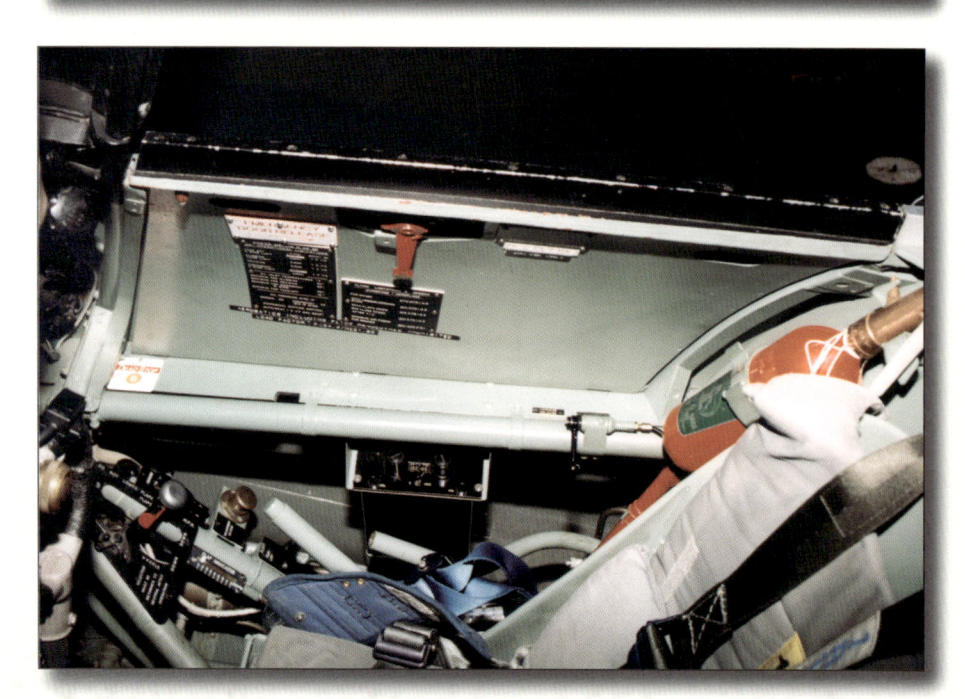

Starboard side of the cockpit. The red fire extinguisher is a modern modification.

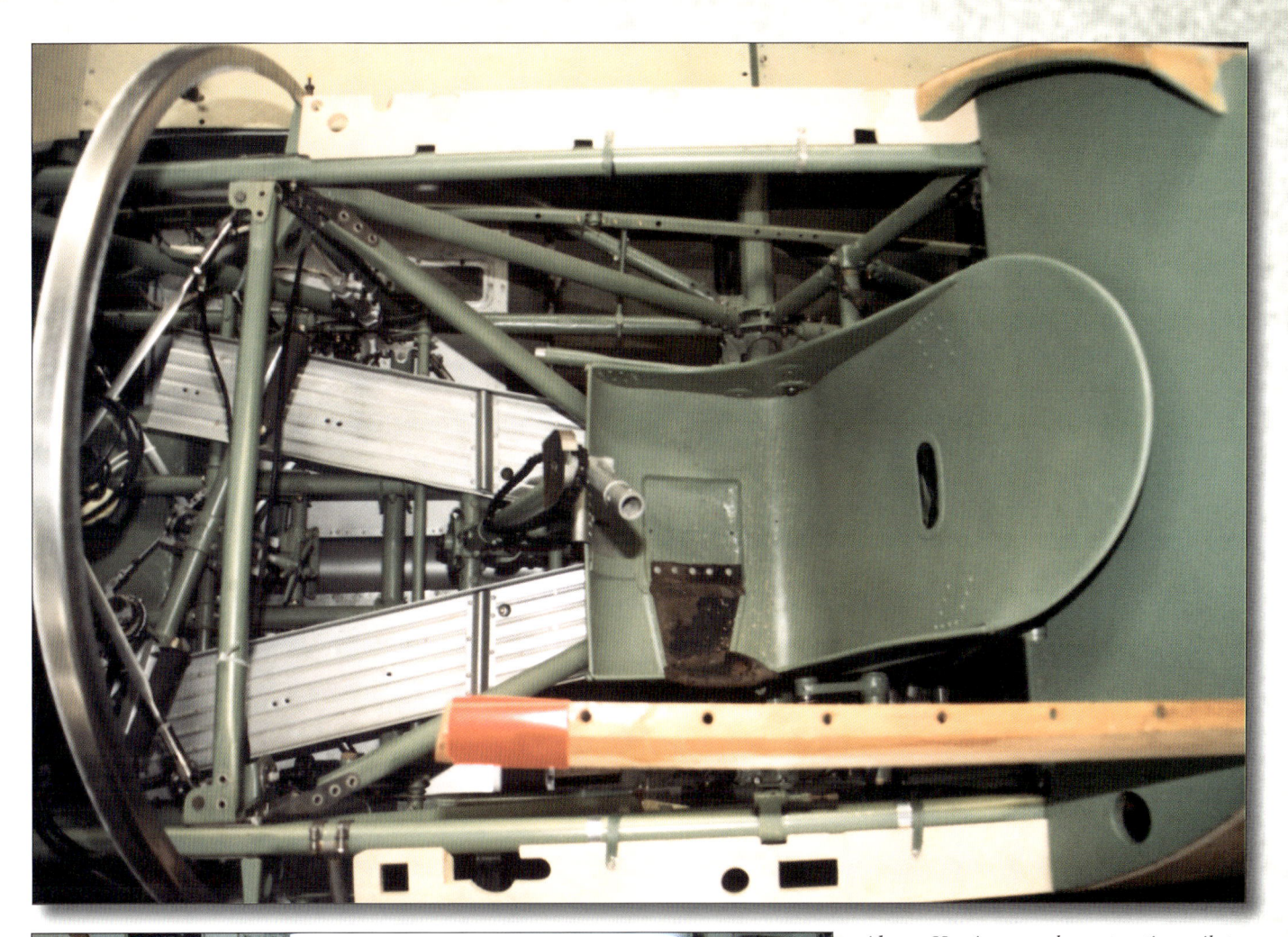

Above: Hurricane under restoration, pilot seat and cockpit wall are visible. (Stratuss coll.)

Left: The wooden skin of the cockpit. (James Kightly)

Below, left: Port side of the cockpit as seen from outside with panel removed. (Stratus coll.)

Below, right: Cockpit as seen from the right via entry hatch. (James Kightly)

Above: Starboard side of the cockpit as seen from outside.

Bottom: Undercarriage and flap selector lever. (Both photos James Kightly)

Above Right: Two photos of the headrest, as required on the Sea Hurricane. (Stratus coll.)

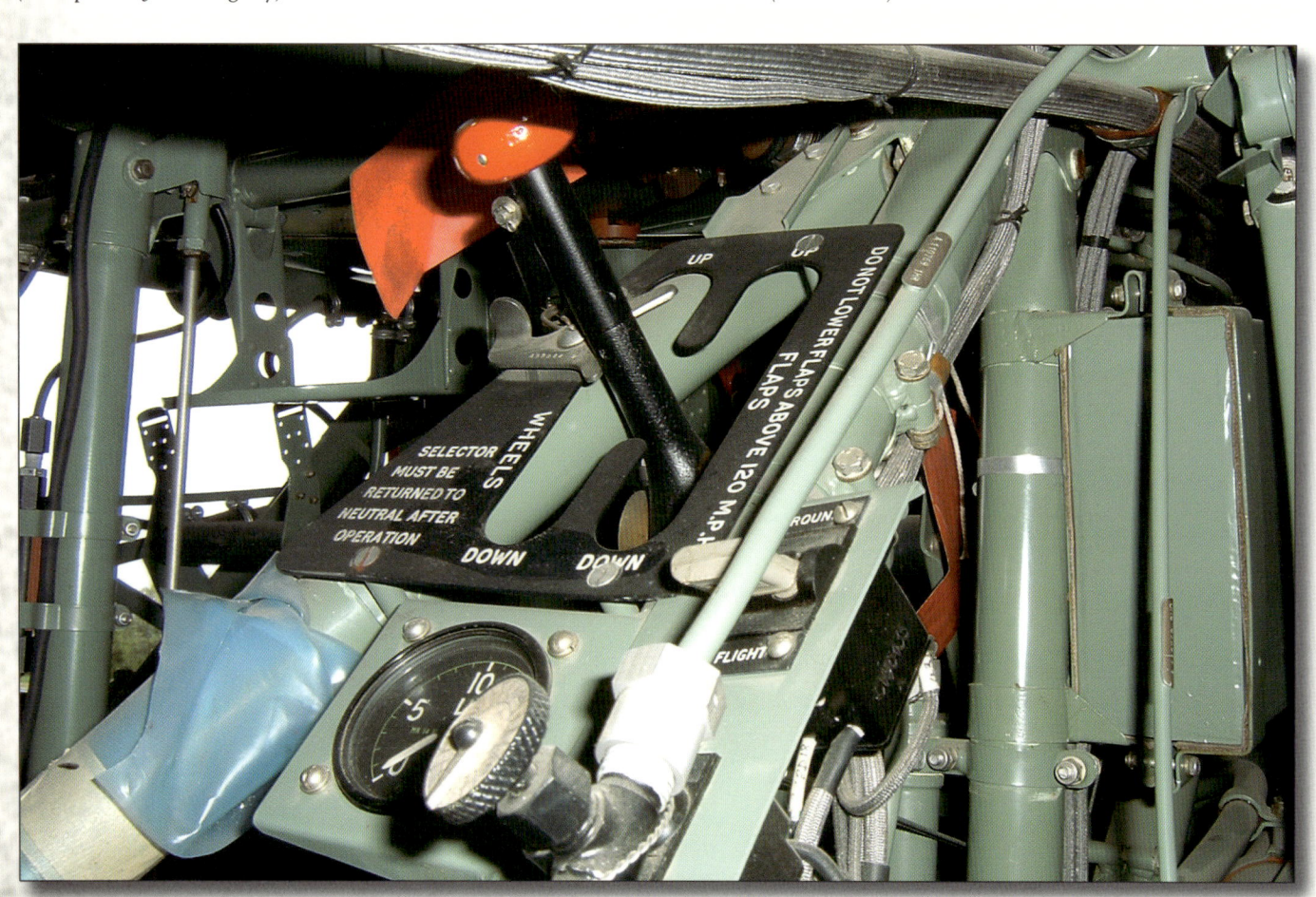

Wing

Right: Undersurface of the Hurricane Mk I wing. (Dariusz Karnas)

Bottom: Uppersurface of the Sea Hurricane wing. (Niall McWilliams)

101

Above: German photo of a destroyed Hurricane in France showing the Hurricane's starboard wing and aileron details. (via Tomasz Kopański)

Details of the starboard aileron on Sea Hurricane. (Stratus coll.)

Bottom: Underside of the port Hurricane Mk I wing. (Martti Kujansuu)

Two photos of the early Hurricane Mk I fabric-covered wing undersurfaces (above) and upper surface (lower). (Stratus coll. & James Kightly)

Right & bottom: *Two photos of the early Hurricane Mk I fabric-covered wing undersurfaces. The patches are museum repairs. (James Kightly & Stratus coll.)*

Below: *Starboard aileron of the Hurricane Mk I with fabric-covered wing. (Stratus coll.)*

This page: Three photos of Hurricane landing flap construction.
In the photos below flaps are in fully open position.
(All photos Stratus coll.)

Above: Starboard, green navigation light. (Martti Kujansuu)

Right: Port side wing tip and red navigation light. (Stratus coll.)

Middle: Close-up view of the port (red) navigation light. (Stratus coll.)

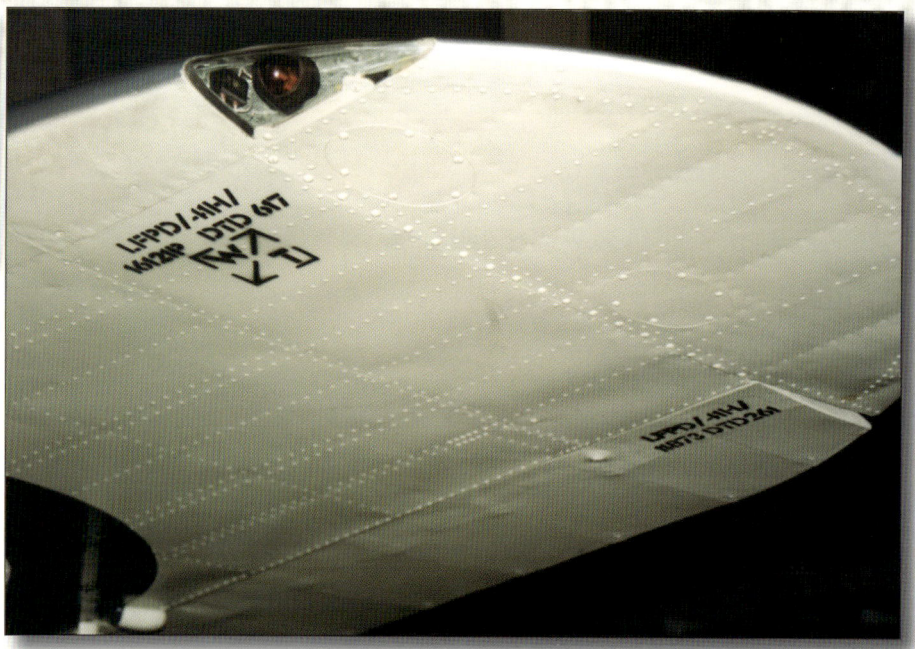

Starboard wing of the Hurricane Mk I. (Dariusz Karnas)

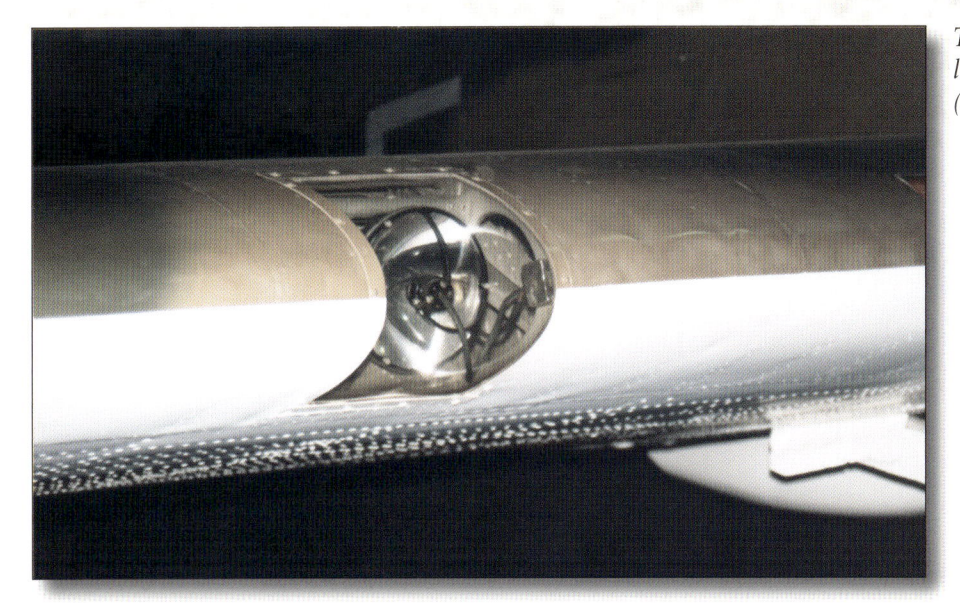

Top & middle: Two photos of the landing light details.
(Stratus coll. & Dariusz Karnas)

Leading edge of the port wing. Note the outer wing panel attachment cover is removed.
(Martti Kujansuu)

107

Pitot tube under the port wing, Hurricane Mk I. (Stratus coll.)

Right: *Leading edge of the port wing. Landing light and pitot tube are visible. (Stratus coll.)*

Below: *Uppersurface of the starboard wing, aileron hinges are visible. (James Kightly)*

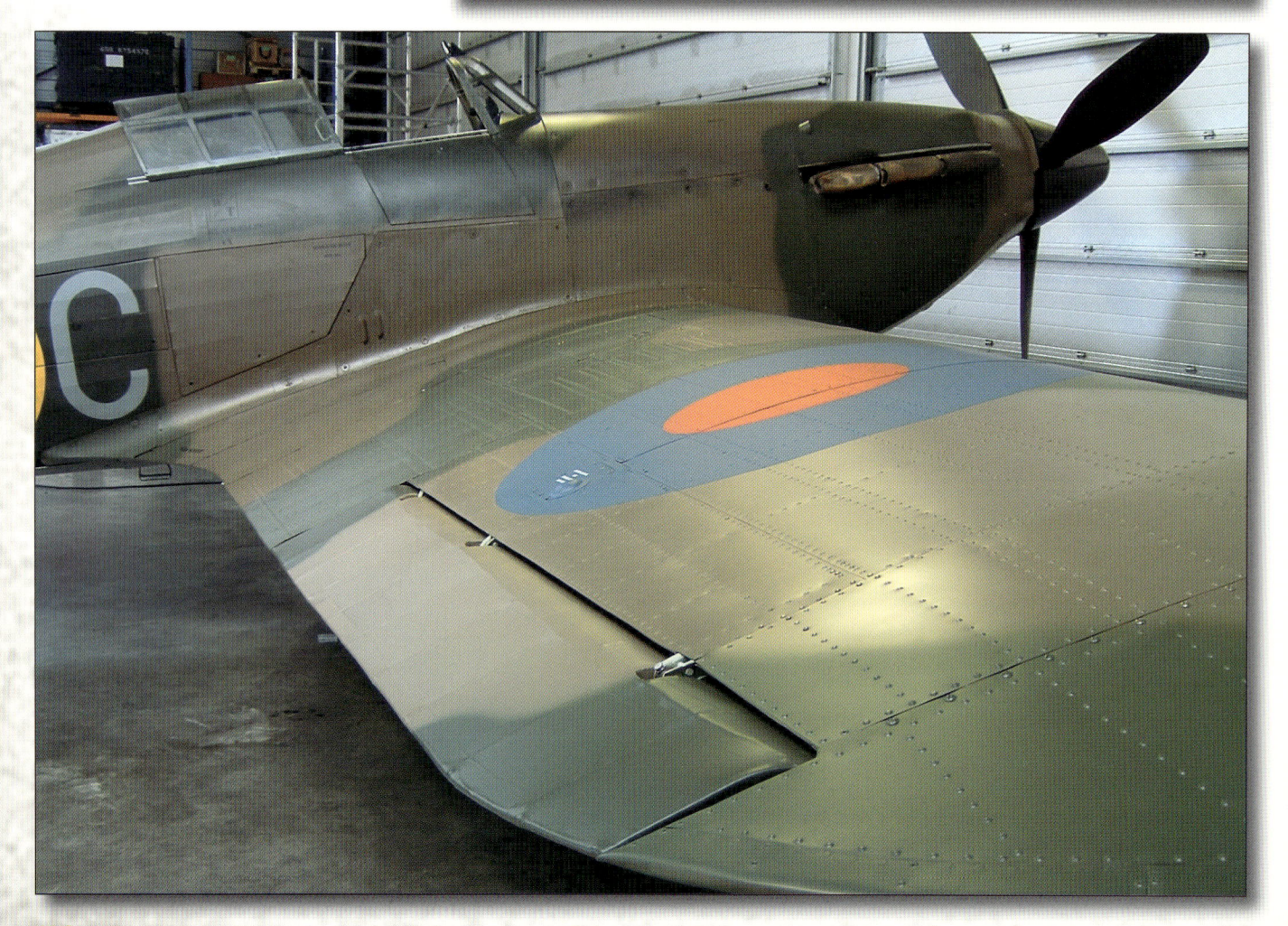

108

Two photos of wing-fuselage fillet seen from below, note the lower formation light.

Inner part of the landing flap seen from below.
(Stratus coll.)

Top, left: Oil tank in the wing, seen from above.

Top, right: Aileron hinge

Right: Oil tank, still without the skin.
(All photos Stratus coll.)

Bottom: Wing rib construction seen during Hurricane restoration.
(Steve Patterson)

Cover of the outer wing panel attachment. Hurricane Mk IV.
(via Przemysław Skulski)

Wing-fuselage fillet, starboard side.

Wing-fuselage fillet port side. Cooling air scoop is also visible.
(Both photos Stratus coll.)

111

Engine

Above: Starboard side of the Hurricane Mk II engine cowling. Note the three stack exhaust. (Dariusz Karnas)
Below: Hurricane with engine cowling removed. Engine with fishtail style exhaust. (James Kightly)

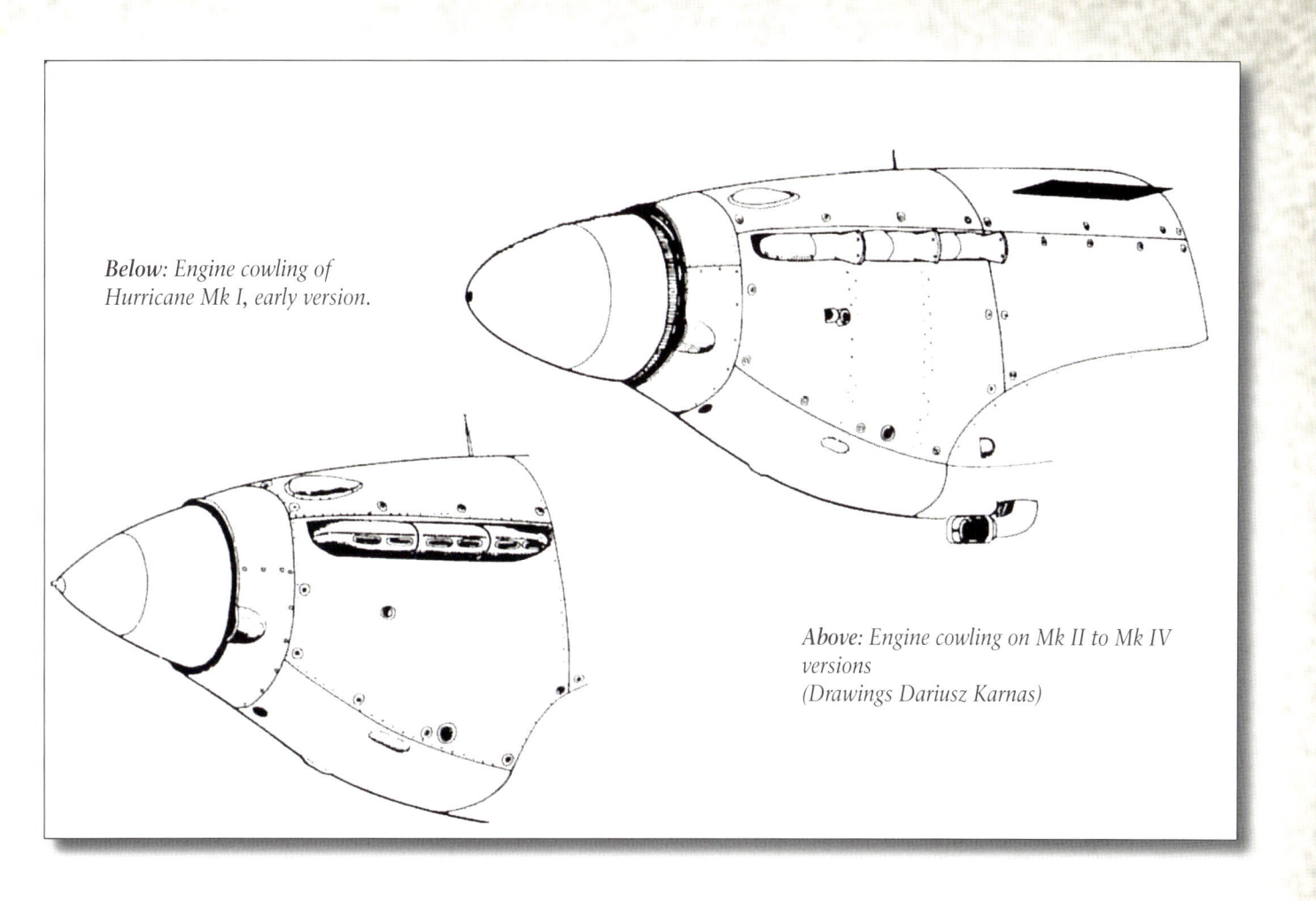

Below: Engine cowling of Hurricane Mk I, early version.

Above: Engine cowling on Mk II to Mk IV versions
(Drawings Dariusz Karnas)

Below: Port side of the Hurricane Mk IIC nose. Fishtail style exhaust stubs. (Stratus coll.)

113

Above: *Wartime photo of the Hurricane Mk I with engine cowling removed. (Stratus coll.)*
Below: *Rolls-Royce Merlin III, 12 cylinder liquid cooled Vee engine prepared for transport. (James Kightly)*

Above: Rolls-Royce engine mounted in the Sea Hurricane. The propeller reduction gearbox is visible.

Below: Sea Hurricane nose with the cowlings and propeller removed. (Both Stratus coll.)

Above: With the engine removed for overhaul, the engine mount structure is visible.

Left: Inverted, the engine mounting framework removed from the aircraft.

Bottom: Wartime photo of a destroyed Hurricane in France, 1940. Details of the engine and fuselage (reserve) fuel tank, capacity 28 Imp gal (127 litre) are visible. (All Stratus coll.)

Above: *Details of the Rolls-Royce engine. Note the engine ducting in different colours. (Stratus coll.)*
Details of the engine with exhaust stubs removed, Engine driven generator (a) and ignition control unit (b) are visible. (Steve Patterson)

117

Firewall with engine mount attached, from three-quarter front view.
Top, left: *Firewall and engine mount – side view. (James Kightly)*

Right: *Exhaust stubs. (Dariusz Karnas)*

Bottom: *3/4 front view of the Hurricane Mk IV with engine cowlings and spinner removed.*
(James Kightly)

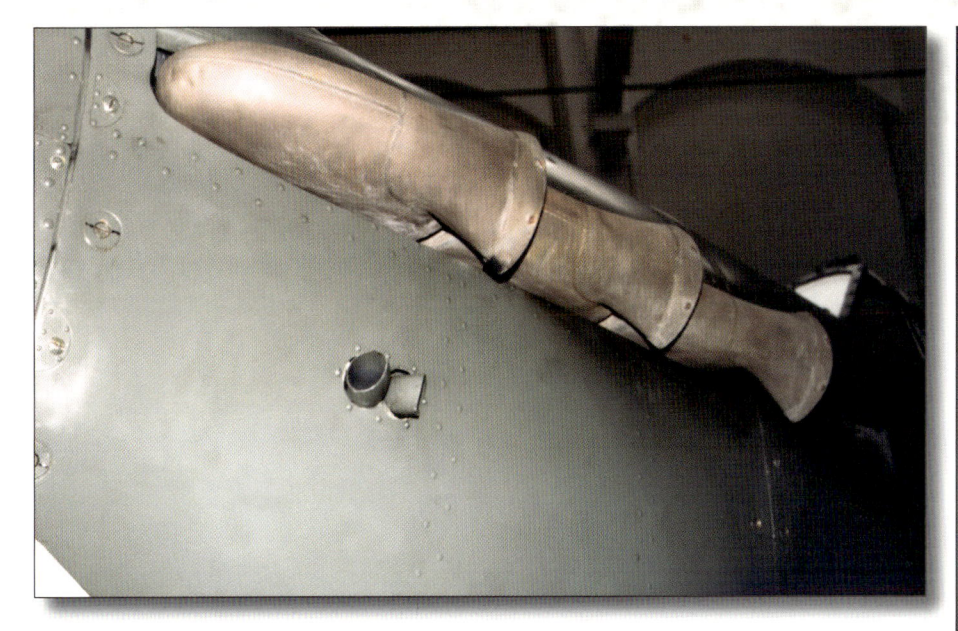

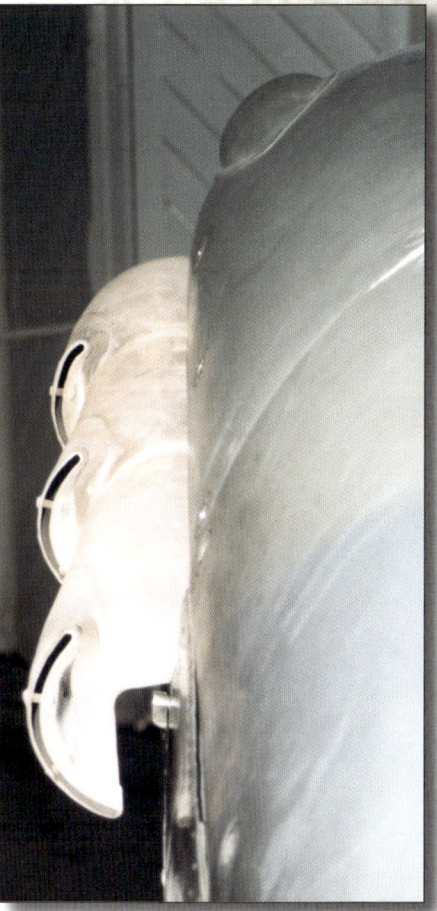

This page: Photos of the fishtail style exhaust stubs. (Stratus coll.)

119

Above: *Starboard side of the early Hurricane Mk I nose. (Stratus coll.)*

Two photos of Hurricane Mk IIC spinner. (Stratus coll.)

Port side of a Canadian Hurricane, showing the distinctive Canadian type flat-tapered spinner. (James Kightly)

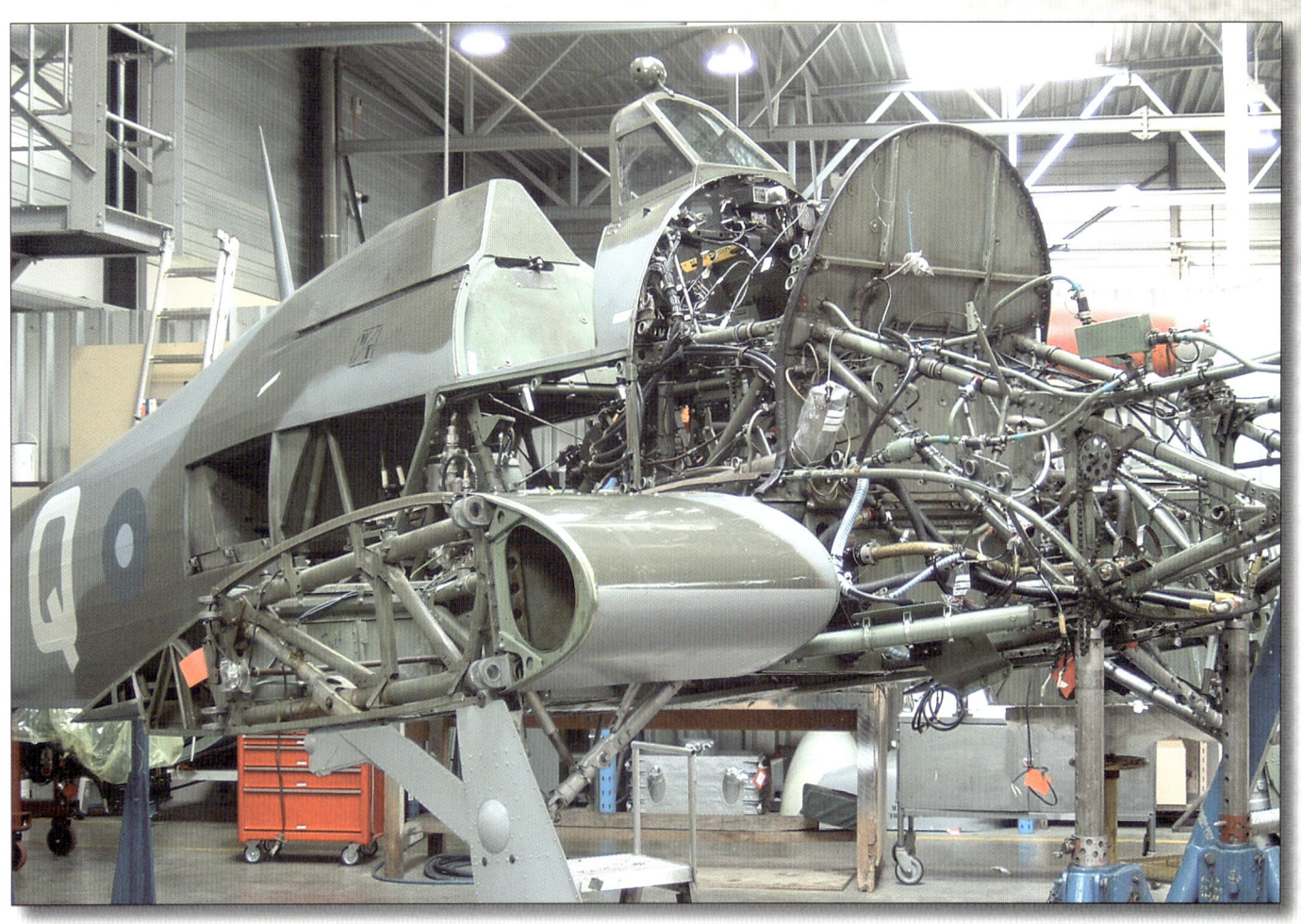

Engine removed showing wiring and pipes. Note also centre wing section strut framework.

Bottom: *Starboard side of the Rolls-Royce engine. (Both photos James Kightly)*

121

Above: Hurricane Mk IIC with engine, side panel removed.

Below: Hurricane under restoration. Engine piping is visible. Note also the front wing spar and undercarriage attachment. (Both photos Steve Patterson)

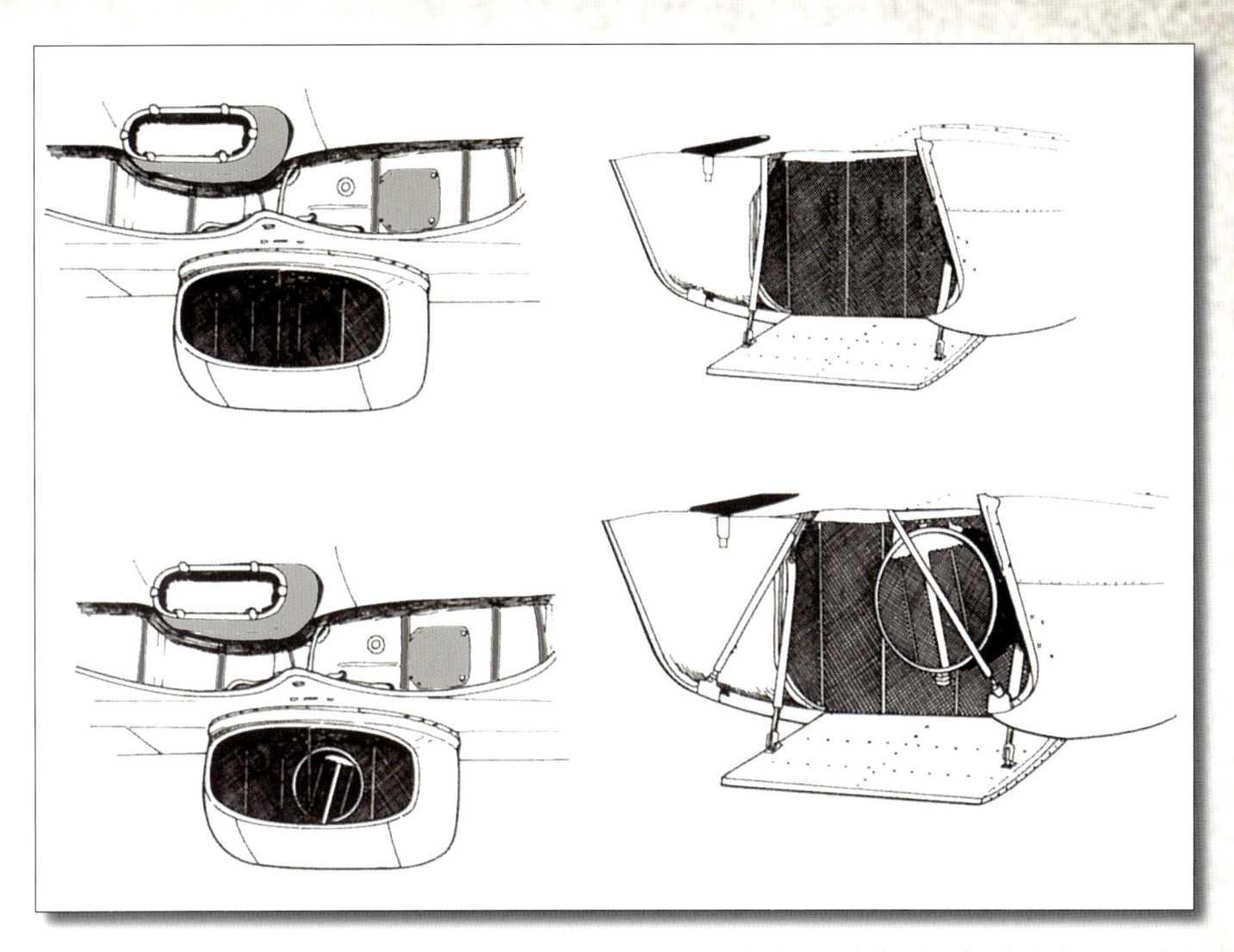

Above: The Hurricane Mk I and Mk II radiators. The Hurricane featured integrated radiator and oil cooler. The Mk I had a rectangular oil cooler, from the Mk II onwards the oil cooler was circular. (Drawings Dariusz Karnas)

Below: Details of the radiator and oil cooler outlet, Hurricane Mk II. (via Przemysław Skulski)

Two photos of the radiator and the oil cooler, front view, Hurricane Mk II. (Straus coll. & Dariusz Karnas)

Radiator of the Sea Hurricane. Note also carburettor air intake. (Stratus coll.)

Port view of the Sea Hurricane radiator. Port catapult spool is also visible. (Stratus coll.)

Front view of the Hurricane Mk I radiator. (James Kightly)

Carburettor air intake on Hurricane Mk I preserved in the Science Museum. (Stratus coll.)

Right & below: *Three photos of the carburettor air intake with Volkes air filter, Hurricane Mk IV. The selector flap for filtered or direct air can be seen inside the intake. (via Przemysław Skulski)*

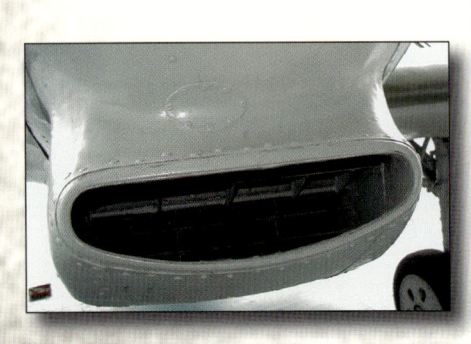

Tail

Starboard side of the Hurricane fabric covered rudder. (James Kightly)

Left: *Port side of the rudder, Hurricane Mk IV.*

Below: *Close-up of the rudder trim tab. (via Przemysław Skulski)*

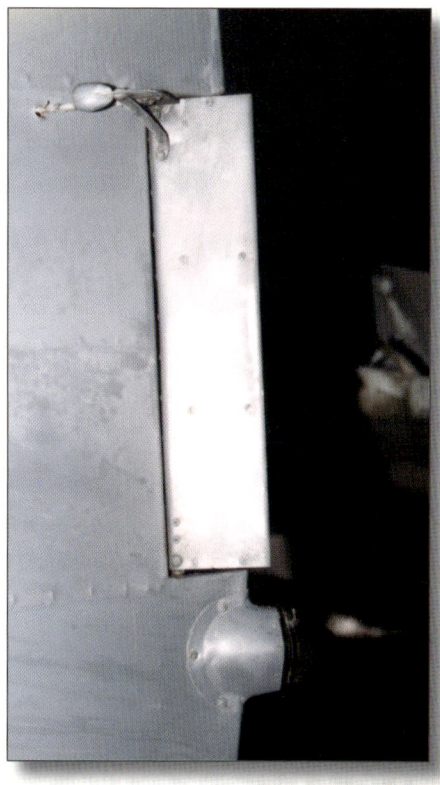

Right & below: *Two photos of the Hurricane Mk I tail. (Martti Kujansuu)*

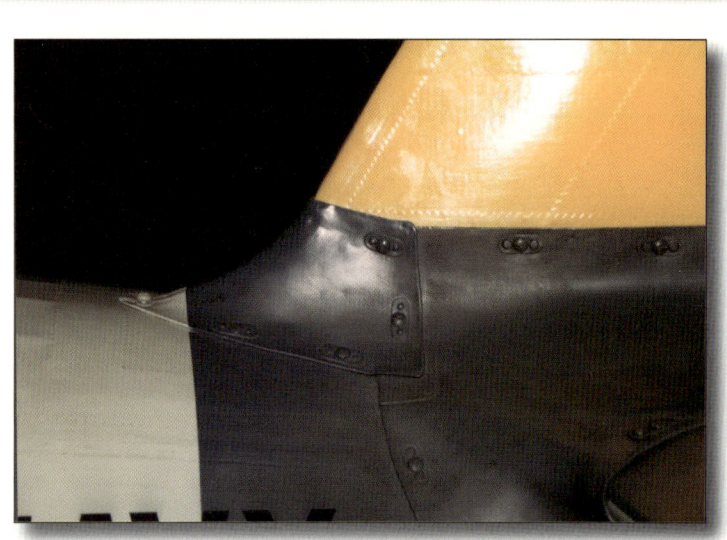

Middle, right: *Fin-fuselage fillet. (Stratus coll.)*

Bottom Right: *Port side of the Hurricane's fin. (James Kightly.)*

128

Left: Rear view of the Hurricane tail.

Below: Rear part of the fuselage framework with tail removed. Note the fin attachment points.

Bottom: Rudder tip with aerial attachment. Rudder upper hinge is also visible. (All James Kightly)

Four photos of the tail construction. Tail was aluminium alloy framework covered by fabric. Note the asymmetric airfoil shape. (All photos James Kightly)

Close-up photo of the early Mk I tailplane construction.
(Stratus coll.)

Two photos of the uppersurface of the horizontal tailplane and elevators.
(All photos Stratus coll.)

Rudder control cables, starboard side

Close-up shot of the rudder trim-tab mass balance.

Rear navigation light.
(All photos Stratus coll.)

Undercarriage

Above: General view of the Hurricane undercarriage. (Dariusz Karnas)

Below: Side view of the main undercarriage. (James Kightly)

133

Main undercarriage of the Finnish Hurricane Mk I. (Martti Kujansuu)

Right: Port main undercarriage leg with covers. (Stratus coll.)

Below: Inner view of the port main undercarriage leg. (Dariusz Karnas)

Above: Two photos of the Hurricane Mk II main undercarriage details. (Stratus coll.)
Below: Inner and outer view of the Hurricane Mk IV main undercarriage leg. Note the non-original mainwheel hub.
(via Przemysław Skulski)

Main wheel well, outside view

Main wheel well. The small rectangular hole in the centre is the inspection opening allowed the pilot to check the undercarriage position.

Main wheel well as seen from the front. (All photos Stratus coll.)

The undercarriage leg retraction strut, normally hidden inside the wing, seen here with the outer wing removed, looking inboard and with the wheels lowered. (James Kightly)

Outboard view of the jack cover. (Stratus coll.)

Leg attachment and the jacks seen from the rear. (Stratus coll)

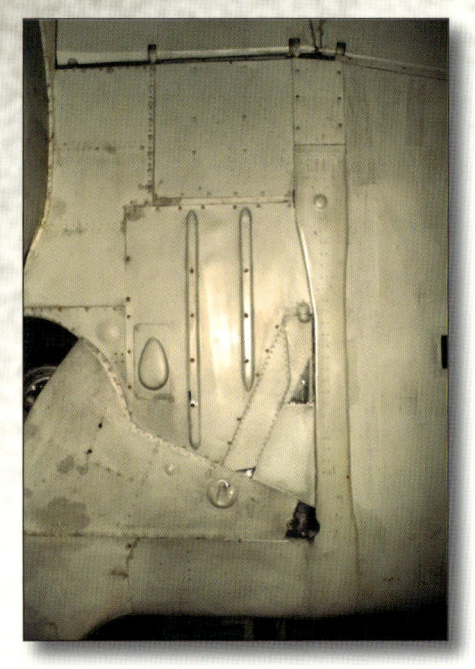

Above: View of the port retracted main undercarriage leg. Hurricane Mk I. (Stratus coll.)

Above, right: Main wheel well of the Hurricane Mk IV. (via Przemysław Skulski)

Right: Main leg and jacks, seen from the rear.

Bottom, right: Main undercarriage in retracted position, Hurricane Mk I. (Both photos Stratus coll.)

Bottom, left: Main wheel, inner view. (Dariusz Karnas)

Photos of early and late (articulated) Hurricane tailwheel forks. (Martti Kujansuu and Stratus coll.)

139

Above, left: Close-up shot of the Hurricane Mk II tailwheel. Shock absorber is visible. (Stratus coll.)

Above, right: Arrestor hook of the Sea Hurricane. (James Kightly)

Below: Front view of the port main undercarriage leg. (James Kightly)

Armament

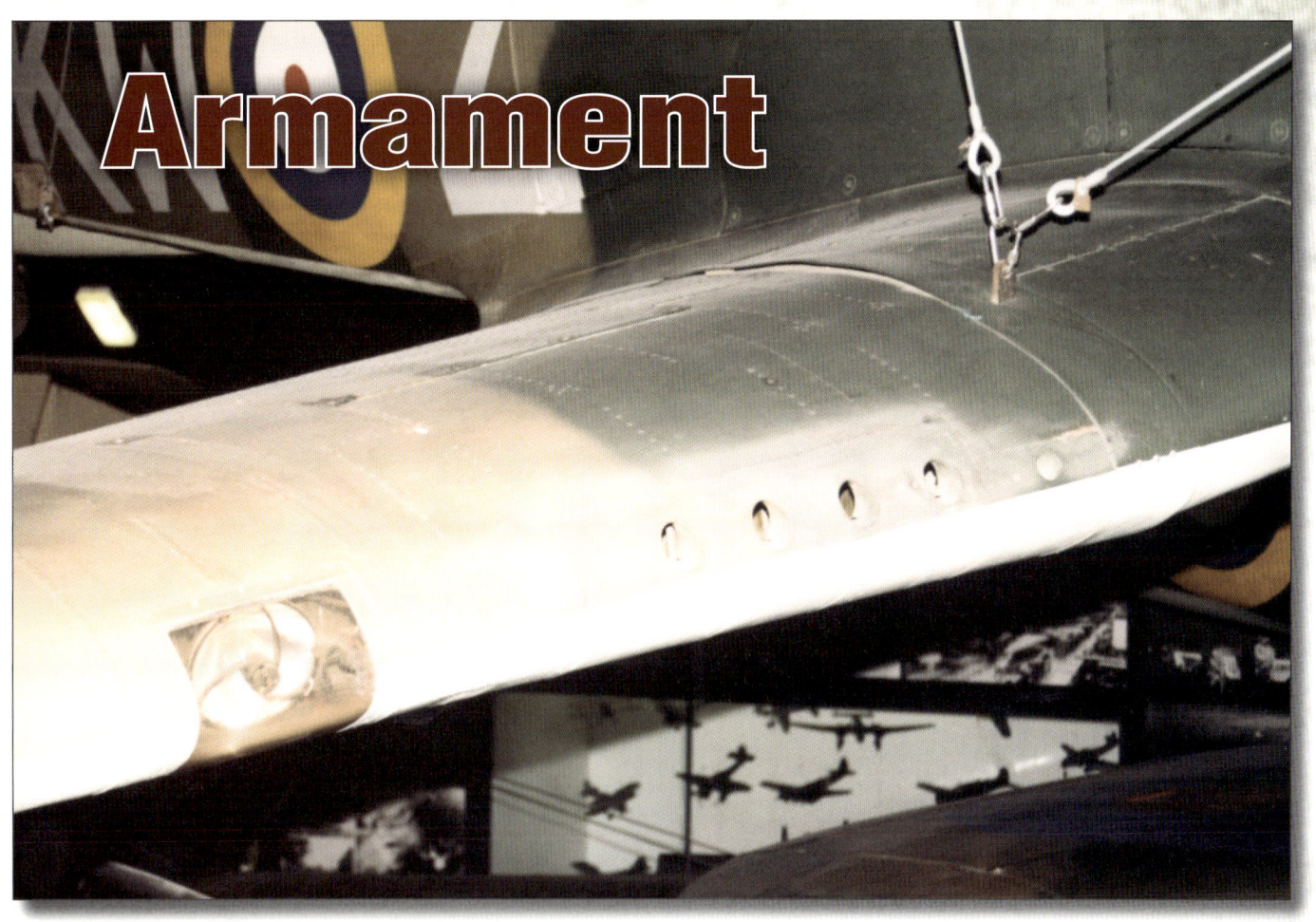

Above: Gun barrel blast tubes of the Hurricane Mk I. (Stratus coll.)
Below: Wartime, German photos of the Hurricane Mk I Browning 0.303 machine guns in the port wing. Ammunition magazines are also visible. (Stratus coll.)

Above: Empty cartridge ejector holes of the Hurricane Mk I. *(Martti Kujansuu)*

Right: The original German drawing showing the arrangement of the Hurricane Mk I armament, armour and fuel tanks.

Below: Wartime photo of Polish fitters checking Brownings on a Polish Squadron Hurricane Mk I. *(Stratus coll.)*

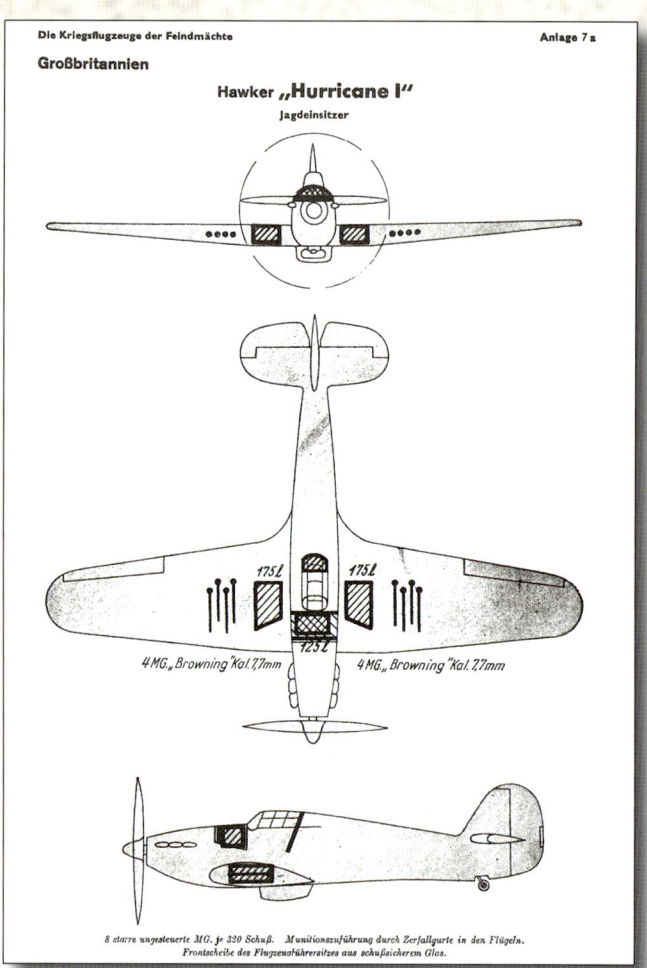

Above and right: Two wartime photos of the rearming of Polish Hurricanes, 1940. (Stratus coll.)

Port gun installation of a metal wing Hurricane Mk I. Note the wing leading edge is on the lower side of the photo (Via Mike Berry)

Wartime photo of the Hurricane Mk IIB armament.
(via Mike Berry)

Close-up photo of the Brownings' flash eliminators as fitted on the 12 gun wing.
(James Kightly)

Above: Hurricane Mk IIC 20 mm cannons in the starboard wing.

Left: The ammunition tanks.

Bottom, left: Close-up view of the Hurricane Mk IIC cannons. Note differences to top photograph.

Bottom, right: Hurricane Mk IIC wing with cannons removed, showing the mounts.

(All photos James Kightly)

Top left: the gun cover removed from a Mk IIC.

Top right: another view of the cannon mounting

Bottom left: the camera gun platform in the inner end of the port wing.
Bottom right: The later, bulged camera gun cover
(James Kightly & via Przemysław Skulski)

Top: Hurricane Mk IID, serial BP188 of 6 Squadron, 1942. (IWM CM 4954)

Middle, left: Rocket for Hurricane at Burma airfield, 1945. (IWM)

Two photos of the rocket attachment under the Hurricane Mk IV wing. (via Przemysław Skulski)

Above: Hurribomber – Hurricane Mk IIC with bomb racks at one of the Burma airfields, 1944. (IWM)

Below: Hurricane Mk IIB with bombs under wings, over Malta. (Stratus coll.)

Survivors

By James Kightly

Notably, at the time of writing, in the UK, for the 75th anniversary of the 18 August 1940 (the Battle of Britain's "Hardest Day') five Hurricanes were flown in a joint formation with Spitfires. This is the greatest number of Hurricanes flying together since the the last operational Hurricanes with the *Força Aérea Portuguesa* and their help filming Angels One Five in 1951. Not even for the Battle of Britain film or even for air displays has this number been operated together in the last sixty years.

While there are a number of further Hurricane "identities" consisting of parts collections or paperwork, and encouragingly several of these are restorations due to fly in the next few years, for the purpose of this book we have focussed on those aircraft that are complete and either on public display, or are displayed at airshows on a regular basis. Much of the data here is based on the work undertaken by Gordon Riley for his new book "Hawker Hurricane Survivors" published by Grub Street. Gordon's researches gives 42 British built examples and 21 Canadian built surviving at the time of publication.

The most exciting development was the recent first flight of Hurricane Mk XII G-CBOE BW874, painted in a Finnish air force scheme as "HC-465" and flown on a tour of Finland in 2014 before reverting to a silver Rhodesian scheme as "AG244", both refreshing changes from the usual. Meanwhile, R4118, G-HUPW, an early Mk I, was recovered from India and flew again shortly before the previous edition's publication. It is still airworthy, with Peter and Polly Vacher, but up for sale at £1,995,000.

Certainly the Hurricanes which have the longest airworthy record, flying since W.W.II, are the Hurricanes of the Battle of Britain Memorial Flight. Based

UK Airworthy

at RAF Coningsby, UK, they operate two Mk IIC Hurricanes which are the only examples still operated by an air force. They are, of course, LF363 which was rebuilt by Historic Flying Ltd. after a crash in 1991, and PZ865 (formerly G-AMAU with Hawker Aircraft) the last Hurricane built, known as "The Last of the Many'.

Also airworthy in the UK are the following, many of which provide some of the detail photographs. Sea Hurricane Mk IB Z7015, G-BKTH with the Shuttleworth Collection, the only surviving Sea Hurricane configured and flown as such. Both Z7015 and R4118 fly with Mk III Merlin engines.

Mk XII 5711, G-HURI, painted as RF-E, "P3700" flies with the Historic Aircraft Collection, Duxford. Hurricane Mk I AE977, built as a Mk Ib, was with Tom Friedkin, in Chino California, but returned to the Biggin Hill Heritage Hangar during 2012, and is painted as "P2921" "GZ-L". Hurricane Mk IIB RCAF 1374 painted as "BE505" (registered G-HHII), is the only example representing the "Hurribomber", being fitted with two underwing bomb racks and is operated by The Hangar 11 Collection, North Weald. Tragically Mk XII 5589, G-HURR was lost in a fatal accident on the 15 September 2007 at Shoreham with its pilot.

G-CBOE, a Hurricane Mk.XII, wears the markings of the Royal Rhodesian Air Force and is based in Germany with new owner K F Grimminger. It's seen here at Goodwood. (Gary R Brown)

Above: Battle of Britain Memorial Flight Hurricane PZ865 has a fiery start at the August 18th, 2015 Biggin Hill event, with P3700 visible behind. (All Gary R Brown)

Right: The Battle of Britain Memorial Flight's Hurricanes, here LF363, regularly have their schemes changed, this being the previous scheme to the one currently worn

Bottom: The Vachers' Battle of Britain veteran Mk I seen in 2006.

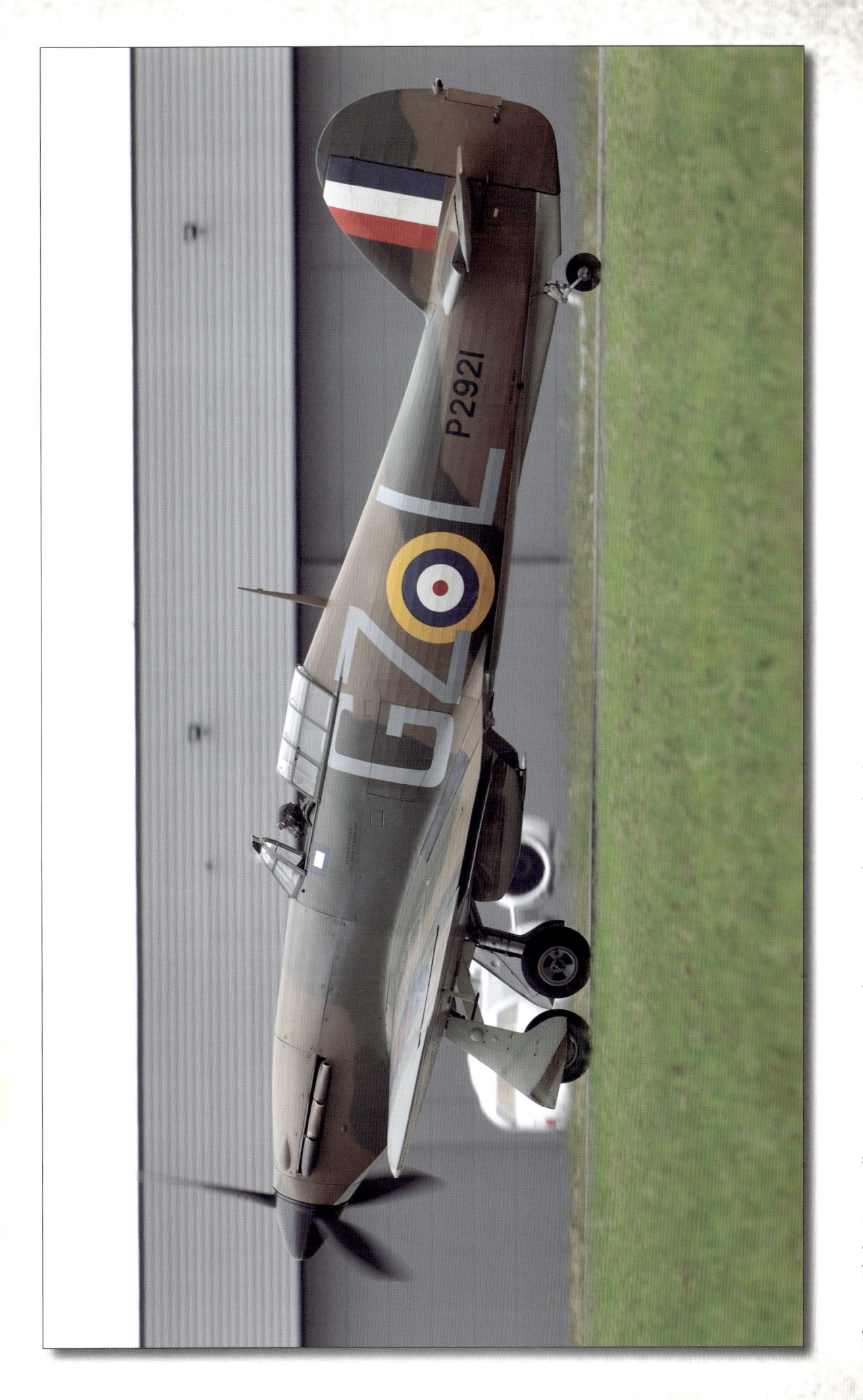

Above: With the Biggin Hill Heritage Hangar, is a Mk I AE977, recently returned to the UK. (Gary R Brown)

Above: Shuttleworth's example is the only Hurricane configured as a Sea Hurricane with hook and catapult spools.

Below: One of the few Hurricanes in a later scheme and role is the Hangar 11 Collection's "Pegs" RCAF 1374 "BE505". (All Gary R Brown)

152

Above: Difficult to see well, but very historic is the oldest surviving Hurricane, L1592, on show at the Science Museum, London.

Below: The RAF Museum's P2671 in the Battle of Britain hall.
(All Gary R Brown)

Above: At the IWM Duxford is the ex-Russian example representing Z2315. *(James Kightly)*

Below: Displayed at Manston with many accessories is LF751. *(Gary R Brown)*

The Flying Heritage Collection example seen outside ready for a display. (James Kightly)

UK Static

The UK has a good variety of static display Hurricanes. The earliest surviving example of all is L1592, is a genuine Battle of Britain survivor, having crash landed at Croydon Airport on 18 August 1940. It is on display in the Science Museum in South Kensington, London. This is the only Hurricane to have its original early fabric wings still fitted. The RAF Museum displays the wreck of P3175 and the complete but hidden in the dark P2617. Additionally there is Mk IIA Z2389 at Brooklands, still being rebuilt; Mk IV KX829, displayed at the Birmingham's "Think Tank" museum, suspended, and painted as Mk I "P3395" "JX•B". Additionally there is Mk IIB painted as "Z2315" "JU•E" at the Imperial War Museum Duxford, then Mk IIC LF738 at RAF Cosford; Mk IIC LF751 RAF Manston painted as "BN230" "FT•A", wreckage of BD731 on show at the Wings Museum at Balcombe, Sussex, and the restoration underway of the early Mk I L1639 at Little Gransden with the Cambridge Fighter & Bomber Society, which can be visited with prior permission.

USA & Canada

In North America there is a reduced number of airworthy Hurricanes. What was G-KAMM, (Sea) Hurricane Mk XIIa, BW881, is now back to its RCAF construction number 5429 as N54FH "Z" and with the Flying Heritage Collection, Seattle, painted in rare and original 135 RCAF Squadron colours. Hurricane Mk XII, 5667, N2549 is with the Fighter Factory, Suffolk, Virginia. Hurricane NX96RW of the Lone Star Flight Museum, Texas, which had just flown before the previous edition's release, was damaged in an accident and further damaged during floods of Hurricane Ike in 2008 in Galveston.

On the ground, non-flying are the superbly restored Mk IIC LF686 at the National Air and Space Museum's Steven F. Udvar-Hazy Center, Washington; and Hurricane XII 5390 representing "Z3174" "XR•B" of 71 Squadron, RAF (one of the Eagle Squadrons) is at the National Museum of the U.S. Air Force, Dayton, Ohio. Additionally, there is Mk XII composite painted in the commemorative (rather than accurate) colours "V6864/DT•A" of Bob Stanford Tuck, on loan at the Pima Air and Space Museum, Tucson, Arizona.

Due to their licence production of the Hurricane, Canada has a large number of the world's survivors to her credit; most overseas, but a significant number also remaining in Canada. Canada's flying Hurricane is Mk IV "KZ321", previously G-HURY, now C-FTPM owned by the Vintage Wings of Canada, at Gatenau, Quebec, and they also have Mk XII 5447 C-GGAJ formerly owned by Harry Whereatt under restoration to also fly. There are the following Mk XII types on show – 5584 at the National Aviation Museum, Rockliffe Ontario; Mk XII 5389 at the Calgary Air & Space Museum, Alberta; 5418 at the Reynolds Pioneer Museum, Wetaskiwin Alberta, and 5461 with the Commonwealth Air Training Plan Museum, Brandon, Manitoba.

Above: Hurricane Mk XII as "Z3174" "XR•B" at the National Museum of the U.S. Air Force, Dayton, Ohio. (Gary R Brown)

Below: Appropriately, as the only other British Commonwealth country to build Hurricanes, in large number, there is an example in Canada's national Collection, the Canadian Aviation & Space Museum. (James Kightly)

The Vintage Wings of Canada example seen when in the UK in 2005. (Gary R Brown)

157

Right: Hurricane Mk IIC LF658 seen in Belgium, under a Canadian-built Bollingbroke. (James Kightly)

Below: Pulling into the vertical is the French based Hurricane F-AZXR, P3351. (Gary R Brown)